Heroes and Zeroes, and a Lum or Two

PERSONALITIES

You gotta call 'em personalities! They're just plain too big ▓▓▓▓▓▓▓▓▓▓▓ Clark, Ly the Fairy—they all live in heroic realms and perform dashing deeds on a ▓▓▓▓▓▓▓▓▓▓▓ p against while ferreting out secrets and treasures are just as big and full of evil. So ▓▓▓▓▓▓▓▓▓▓▓

Rayman, our hero! For a guy without arms and legs hands and feet, he really gets things done. He can fly on a limited basis and has a powerful punch.

Globox, Rayman's intrepid friend. Strong as an ox and about as intelligent. Globox starts out with an ability to hide things in his big mouth, then he learns a magical rain dance that really comes in handy.

Ly, the fairy. A good and trusted friend of Rayman's. She has an assortment of magical powers.

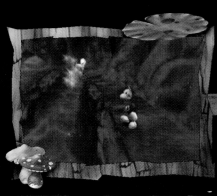

The Murfy brothers, an acquaintance of Rayman's. He provides a lot of information at important times.

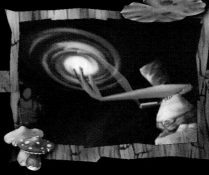

Polokus, the master of the four masks who will use his magic to ultimately defeat Captain Razorbeard. He can only help you when he's at full strength, and to get there you'll have to find all four masks for him.

The Teensies, denizens you must save when you visit various realms. They offer little in the way of help, but they are hilarious to see in action.

Ssssam the Swamp Snake. One of Rayman's pals. You'll need to find and free him in the Marshes of Awakening to get him to help you.

Clark. Here's one of Rayman's more powerful friends, but he can be a little dense. However, his ability to walk through walls can come in quite handy.

Carmen the Whale. She's great big and beautiful. Underwater, she's also a life-saver and gives you the ability to swim on to the next phase of your adventure—if you stick close to her!

Uglette, Globox's charming wife. Rayman will have to rescue her dozens of children to repair her broken heart.

Baby Globoxes. At first, all it seems that they want is their dad back, but by the end of the game, they're going to be in as much trouble as anyone.

Captain Razorbeard, Rayman's evil nemesis. He's a villain with plans, and a large crew and plenty of ships to carry those plans out. He'll stop at nothing.

Robo-pirates are the scourge of the places Rayman has to save. They're mean and evil, and really good shots if given the chance. Don't give them the chance.

These robo-pirates are pretty much indestructible. They are placed as guards over secret or important areas. You will have to find a clever way to get around them.

The barrel-shaped robo-pirates are incredibly tough and doubly dangerous. Use ricochet shots to put them away, or avoid them altogether.

Axel, the icicle-throwing guardian of the Sanctuary of Water and Ice.

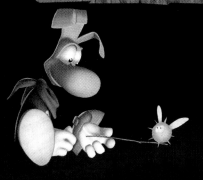

Umber, the guardian of the Sanctuary of Lava and Fire. He's not a real threat, but you'll have to figure out his secret, then avoid letting him lead you to your death.

Foutch, the Guardian of Stone and Rock, throws deadly lava bursts. Avoid him and use his own terrain against him to get the third mask.

The Grolgoth, the ultimate weapon Razorbeard uses against Rayman. The big suit of armor is virtually indestructible, but it has its weak spots.

Walking shell. When the walking shell first sees you, it tries to destroy you. Exhaust it by running away from it but staying almost within reach. Then mount it and ride it to places you couldn't get to without it.

Lums, Lums, Magical Lums

Yellow Lums are scattered throughout the places you have to visit. Collect all 1000!

Yellow Lum Five-Pack. Sometimes the yellow Lums come in groups of five, making them much easier to collect in a hurry. They also come with a lot of personality. See the big smile?

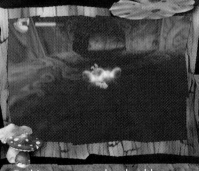

Red Lums restore lost health.

Blue Lums give you extra breath under water.

Green Lums save your progress in the game.

Purple Lums provide ring-shaped supports that allow Rayman to throw his magic fist and swing across large distances.

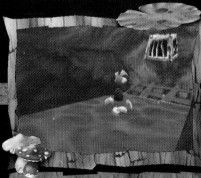

Find the pirate cages and break them open to free the contents inside. Sometimes it will be Lums, Teensies, or other goodies.

Heroes and Zeroes, and a Lum or Two

The Woods of Light

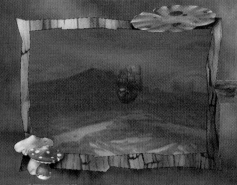

The quest begins aboard the evil pirate ship, *Buccanneer* where Rayman is being held prisoner.

Ly, Rayman's fairy friend, has sent help. Unfortunately, that help doesn't appear very helpful!

Here's our hero, stuck behind the electrified bars of his cell down in the pirate ship hold.

Still, when Rayman sees Globox, he's happy to have the company.

Rayman sorrowfully explains that his powers have left him and he really can't save the world this time around.

Then Globox tells Rayman that Ly sent a gift that will help them. Globox opens his mouth and reaches down his throat to get the silver Lums there.

The magic swirls around Rayman, powering him back up.

Energized again, Rayman immediately begins looking for a way out.

Rayman spots a potential escape route at the back wall.

Press Ⓑ to pop your magic fist out and batter the screen off the pipe. Instant escape route!

Leave your cell through the pipe.

Begin the long slide to freedom.

Catch as many of the five red Lums as you can on your way down to bring your life level up.

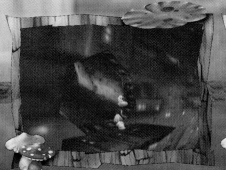

You come to a brief stop on a ledge.

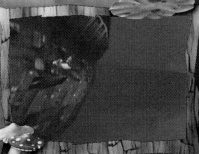

But Globox is *right* behind you in the pipe. Then he's right on top of you!

After the long plummet to the earth, you're not much worse for wear. After all, you're Rayman and you have a world to save!

Globox seems to be missing, though.

Turn around to find the stone on the wall. These are going to be important later in the game to announce warp gates to the Hall of Doors so learn to look for them.

In the distance, you can hear someone screaming for help. Could it be Globox? As you face the sign, a bridge lies off to your left.

Cross the bridge.

Follow the path under the waterfall on the right.

The Woods of Light

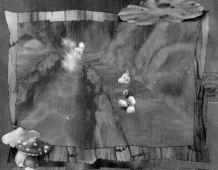

A little farther on, you're joined by Murfy, who's going to be your guide.

Murfy tells you about the carved stones. He says it's a magic stone that can read your thoughts. They're there to help you. Go stand on the magic stone to get the instructions there.

In front of you, another stone sign hangs on the wall. That's the stone you saw earlier.

Turn to the right of the magic stone and follow the water through the tunnel ahead.

Only a short distance into the tunnel, you spot a pirate cage hanging by a chain from the ceiling.

Throw your magic fist at the pirate cage twice to smash it open and free the yellow Lum inside.

Grab the yellow Lum.

NOTE

Once you have a yellow Lum, press Ⓛ to see the secrets it'll give you.

INGENIOUS

Yellow Lums are the 1,000 fragments of primordial core that was broken by the robo-pirates. They contain universal knowledge. The more you gather, the more you'll learn. You can access the secrets of the world by pressing Ⓛ. Find 49 Lums to advance.

Immediately, a trap door opens beneath you.

Follow the water forward through another tunnel.

TIP

You can point the camera with Z, C▲, C▼, C◄, *and* C►.

Another magic stone is ahead and to the right in the clearing that the tunnel lets out onto. Go see what this magic stone has to offer.

Hop on the ledges ahead and to the left of the stream.

Turn to the right and hop on the next ledge to grab your second yellow Lum.

Once you have the yellow Lum, turn around and leap to the ledges by the magic stone. Follow the ledges up to the third yellow Lum.

Take the yellow Lum and meet the inquisitive dragonfly creature that investigates you.

TIP

Hang on to the walls whenever you can.

Wade through the water to find the next magic stone.

Walk through the stream to the waterfall at the end to find your fourth yellow Lum.

Return to the magic stone and leap up on the ledge to the right.

Follow this ledge forward to the next magic stone.

Run, then jump as high as you can while standing at the edge of the ledge. Press Ⓐ to start your super chopper. Glide over to the three strange-looking creatures by the tunnel mouth.

The Woods of Light

It doesn't take you long to figure out these are Globox's kids and they miss him terribly. Of course, it's all your fault poor old Globox is missing.

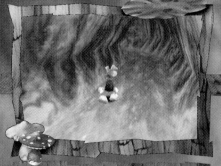

After promising to save their dad, and to help Ly, who has been kidnapped by the robo-pirates, take off through the new tunnel.

In the clearing ahead, stay to the right.

Go through the doorway into the next clearing. The cries for help continue.

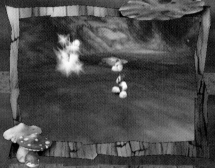

Stay to the left to find another magic stone that brings Murfy to you.

Climb up the walls using Ⓐ; grab the fifth yellow Lum between the walls.

Walk through the opening at the top of the walls and spot the next pirate cage hanging from the tree ahead.

Break open the pirate cage. Instead of getting a yellow Lum this time, you get four interesting fellows.

Each of them claims to be king of the Teensies. But when you ask them about Ly, they tell you that the robo-pirates have taken Ly to the Fairy's Glade and locked her in one of their castles. You'll have to go to the Hall of Doors to get started after her.

They prepare the gate to the Hall of Doors for you and you jump in.

CAUTION
Until you have all five yellow Lums on this level you won't be allowed to go any farther!

8

The Fairy Glade

Here you are at the Hall of Doors. Use the joystick controller to move the Lum to the correct door. Choose the Fairy Glade.

NOTE

With this function in the game, you don't have to find every yellow Lum on every level before getting to move on. You can find the entry point to the next level, then go back at a later time to get all the Lums from past levels and completely beat the game.

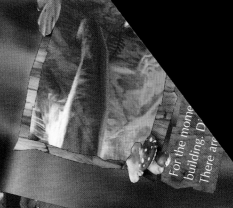

For the mome building. D There ar

dumps you b
Doors, so leave it alone.

Cross the bridge ahead and aim for the red Lum on the ledge. Stop on the island and bounce on

the purple mushroom to grab the yellow Lum ahead. You'll also find you can hang from the yellow path overhead. For now, drop back down.

NOTE

Remember: Red Lums restore your health.

Jump and glide over from the island to the right-hand ledge toward the red Lum.

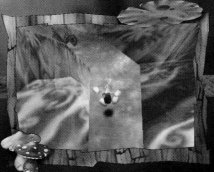

Go up the ledge and grab the red Lum.

You can't get to the red Lum here yet, but you do meet some interesting creatures standing in front of the doorway. You get even more bad news: the doorway is locked.

The Fairy Glade

RAYMAN 2
THE GREAT ESCAPE

NOTE

To swim, use the joystick. To dive, press Ⓩ. To resurface, press Ⓐ.

...t, don't enter this ...ve into the water first. ...some secrets to discover.

Keep the main wall to your left, not the foundation of the island where you got the yellow Lum, and swim forward. Spot the blue Lum ahead.

TIP

Blue Lums give you air while you swim long distances under water. The blue Lums also reappear almost instantly, so you can backtrack for a breath of air. You'll even find some that you can swim through again and again. But remember to surface when you need to or you'll drown!

Swim inside the tunnel by the blue Lum.

At the back of this underwater cavern is another pirate cage.

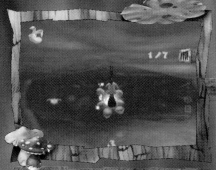

Break the pirate cage open and free the Lum inside.

Return through the tunnel and go back to the island where the purple mushroom is.

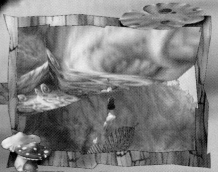

Bounce on the mushroom and hang onto the elevated path.

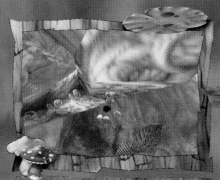

Crawl along the elevated path in the direction of the red bush.

Drop down onto the ledge ahead.

Follow the trail ahead.

Find a yellow Lum waiting around one of the corners.

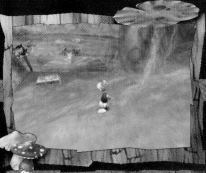

The magic stone ahead says swimming isn't advised. Don't jump in.

Jump across the lily pads but look out for the piranha jumping back and forth in the water. You can disintegrate it with your magic fist if you want to.

Once you make it across all the lily pads, you'll find a red Lum over another magic stone.

Follow the ledge where you got the red Lum to the back wall. You'll find smaller ledges on the right that lead up the wall.

Leap up the ledges.

Once you make it to the corridor at the end of the ledges, follow it around.

Cross the rope bridge.

Throw your magic fist into the red switch ahead.

Once the red switch is thrown, a door farther on opens. This is the locked door you found earlier.

The Fairy Glade

Turn to the left and collect the yellow Lums along the gnarled branch.

When you come to the fork in the path, head to the left first.

At the top of the branch is a house with a pirate cage hanging from it.

TIP

The waterfall splashing across the branch makes the going very slippery. You might want to jump over the water.

Throw your magic fist at the pirate cage to break it.

Jump up to hit the cage with your magic fist. The yellow Lum will come to you, so don't go getting all acrobatic when you don't need to.

Return to the fork and take the other path. Jump off and get the red Lum hanging in the air here. This is the red Lum you couldn't get earlier.

Enter the doorway ahead where Globox's kids are.

Follow the corridor to find a green Lum and another magic stone.

TIP

Take the green Lums. If you die, you'll reappear where you last took one.

Follow the ledge down under the waterfall.

There are a number of interesting devices in the next area.

And look! Another piranha sign. Take a dip and you're duck soup!

Follow the ledge around to the left.

Ahead, a giant pipe spews nasty glop into the water. No wonder the fish are biting!

Go down to the rope bridge.

Go up the rope bridge.

Climb up on the pipe.

Walk through the little room at the top, following the walkway.

When the walkway comes to a sudden end, you've got a couple of options. You could jump to the next walkway beside you, or you could go investigate that big floating barrel in the water below.

For now, choose the barrel and glide down to the ledge beside it. From the ledge, hop onto the barrel.

Once you're on the barrel, it starts moving.

The circuit the barrel takes gets you another yellow Lum as well as two red ones.

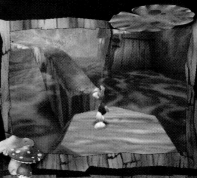

When the barrel stops, turn around to find the ledge leading back up to the small room. Glide over to it.

The Fairy Glade

Walk back up the rope bridge and through the small room. Leap onto the other walkway this time.

Walk up to the pump section.

Grab the red Lum by the pumps.

Leap onto the shorter pump first. Then leap onto the next pump and onto the ledge from there.

CAUTION

Timing really matters a lot when you're working with the pumps. Also, make certain you don't fall into the water because whatever's being pumped into it will kill you instantly.

Follow the next cavern out. Look to the left of the tree ahead to find a red Lum. But look out for the purple caterpillar!

TIP

The caterpillar makes the same journey around in this area every time, so it's really easy to avoid.

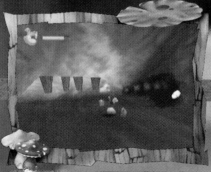

A fence below blocks any escape from this area.

Because there's no returning to where you entered from, go back to the side of the tree where you found the red Lum and start climbing.

Keep climbing up and around the tree.

At the top of the climb, drop off onto the branch and walk to the ledge.

A waterfall lies ahead.

Slide down the waterfall and collect the red Lums along the way to restore your health.

Follow the corridor all the way to the end to find a yellow and red Lum hanging near to each other. Take them both.

The building to the left has a pirate cage in it, but you have to get over there first.

NOTE

Getting to the pirate cage here is actually a secret. You won't be able to get to it from here. Once you get to the Echoing Caves level, there's a secret entrance that will bring you back here.

A waterfall with a leaping piranha is to the right.

And here on the wall are the gnarly vines you need to climb around on.

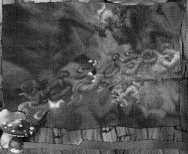

Climb the vines and work your way around the piranha.

Grab the red Lum only a little farther on.

Once you have the red Lum, go back and leap up onto the vines above.

Avoid the piranha and make your way around the vines through the waterfall to find another red Lum.

Keep following the vines to get a yellow Lum.

For the moment there's still no way to get to that building where the pirate cage is. But you can see that interesting rope ladder near the top now.

The Fairy Glade

Turn around and follow the passage-way here through the hills.

A sinister building sits up ahead.

An even more sinister creature is watching out over it—watching you!

Approach the building but avoid the flaming catapult loads.

Run to the left and follow the ledge up to the building.

On the left beside the building is a tunnel.

Enter the tunnel and follow it around.

Ahead is another piranha pond. But this one also has a yellow Lum sitting on one of the lily pads. Tempting, huh?

Kill the piranha with your magic fist, then leap across the lily pads to get the yellow Lum.

Start with the lily pad farthest to the right in this area where another yellow Lum is.

Glide to the center lily pad and get the yellow Lum there. Glide to the next lily pad to get the yellow Lum there. Then glide to the ledge and take the ladder up, getting the yellow Lum as you go by.

Three red Lums flutter on the ledge above.

Climb up the nearby ladder and see where it leads.

Follow the ledge around toward the waterfall ahead.

Cross the bridge over the waterfall.

Throw your magic fist at the pirate cage ahead.

Jump up to hit the pirate cage.

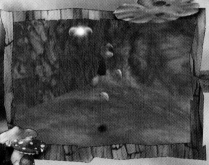

Jump up again to the left to get the yellow Lum.

You still can't get to the last pirate cage inside the building you had to leave behind.

Return through the tunnel under the waterfall that brought you into this area. Drop through the square hole in the ground in front of the pirate fortress.

On the ramp below, stare out at the line of crates floating in the green water. Don't enter the water or you'll die.

The Fairy Glade

Use your chopper ability to float from crate to crate. Judge if you're over them by watching your shadow. Gather the Lums along the way.

Jump to the left at the end of the crates to find a green Lum on a ledge.

Watch out for the falling barrels and climb the cobweb on the wall.

The second part of the web gets harder. Dodge back and forth on the web to avoid the falling powder kegs. Watch the doors open to signal you which way to go.

Use the opening doors above as warnings.

TIP

At this point, go slowly. You can cover a big distance if you can get to the top even if you only make it by inches at a time. Also, if you get knocked loose from the wall, activate the chopper and glide back to the web so you don't fall all the way down and die.

Grab onto the ledge and pull yourself up.

Throw your magic fist into the door to break it down.

Coming up this way, you've managed to sneak up on the robo-pirate in his fortress.

When you reach the top of the steps to get the green Lum there, Murfy shows up to warn you about the robo-pirates ahead.

TIP

Use Z to move around during combat and to keep your enemy targeted.

Move around quickly and keep the robo-pirates targeted with your magic fist. You have to hit them a lot to knock them out.

TIP

The red Lums are on a timer here, so move quickly. You'll find that when the game is being generous with the extra health, you'll have to move fast to reap the rewards.

Climb up the nearby ladder and see where it leads.

Follow the ledge around toward the waterfall ahead.

Cross the bridge over the waterfall.

Throw your magic fist at the pirate cage ahead.

Jump up to hit the pirate cage.

Jump up again to the left to get the yellow Lum.

You still can't get to the last pirate cage inside the building you had to leave behind.

Return through the tunnel under the waterfall that brought you into this area. Drop through the square hole in the ground in front of the pirate fortress.

TIP

You have to lure one of the catapult loads onto the door covering the square hole in the ground to break it open.

On the ramp below, stare out at the line of crates floating in the green water. Don't enter the water or you'll die.

TIP

Make use of your shadow and helicopter.

The Fairy Glade

17

Use your chopper ability to float from crate to crate. Judge if you're over them by watching your shadow. Gather the Lums along the way.

Jump to the left at the end of the crates to find a green Lum on a ledge.

Watch out for the falling barrels and climb the cobweb on the wall.

The second part of the web gets harder. Dodge back and forth on the web to avoid the falling powder kegs. Watch the doors open to signal you which way to go.

Use the opening doors above as warnings.

TIP

At this point, go slowly. You can cover a big distance if you can get to the top even if you only make it by inches at a time. Also, if you get knocked loose from the wall, activate the chopper and glide back to the web so you don't fall all the way down and die.

Grab onto the ledge and pull yourself up.

Throw your magic fist into the door to break it down.

Coming up this way, you've managed to sneak up on the robo-pirate in his fortress.

When you reach the top of the steps to get the green Lum there, Murfy shows up to warn you about the robo-pirates ahead.

TIP

Use *to move around during combat and to keep your enemy targeted.*

Move around quickly and keep the robo-pirates targeted with your magic fist. You have to hit them a lot to knock them out.

The Fairy Glade

TIP

Every time you knock a robo-pirate out, a red Lum will be left behind. Rush over to grab it.

There's an open door ahead on the right that the robo-pirate came through. Enter it.

A robo-pirate is asleep against the back wall.

When you get close enough, the robo-pirate wakes up. Use your magic fist to pound him!

TIP

Another interesting tactic to use with the robo-pirate here is to get a powder keg and heave it at him while he's sleeping. Kerblooie! No more robo-pirate.

Grab the ladder that comes down when the robo-pirate goes away.

Climb the ladder and through the ropes strung across the ceiling to get the two yellow Lums.

Make your way to the doorway to the right of the ladder.

Notice a switch on the wall above a deadly trap below you.

Hit the switch to open the door above it.

For the moment, drop back down into the room with the ladder. Go get the powder keg against the wall on the right.

Pack the powder keg outside to the locked door in the area where you first encountered a robo-pirate.

Throw the powder keg at the plank-bandaged door to blow it open.

Enter the doorway and go down the steps.

Turn to the right to find the pirate cage you saw earlier. Use your magic fist to break it open.

Get the five Lums inside.

Return to the room with the ladder and climb up.

If you happen to fall into the room with the trap below, the net acts like a trampoline. To get out, bounce and get close to the doorway you opened.

Turn right and hop through the electrified bars ahead.

Wait until the top bar is on its way up and leap across the lower bar.

Go down the steps and follow the corridor.

Just ahead, another robo-pirate sleeps beside a switch. Use your magic fist on him to make him go away, then hit the switch to open a door below.

Hop over the railing and enter the open door instead of following the corridor.

Follow this corridor down.

The Fairy Glade

Time the moving electrified bars ahead and leap over them to get through. Go through the corridor ahead.

Two doorways lie ahead.

Turn left and get the yellow Lum there. Another yellow Lum is right below.

Ly the fairy is trapped in a force field in the middle of this clearing.

Enter the doorway to the left of the rope ladder.

Follow the corridor to a green Lum and a powder keg.

TIP

To throw the powder keg high, press Ⓐ. To throw it forward, press Ⓑ.

Pick up the powder keg and head for the big machine in the distance.

Before you get very far, the machine launches an explosive at you.

Use Ⓐ to throw the powder keg high into the air.

Stand your ground and use your magic fist to detonate the explosive.

NOTE

Every time you need it, another powder keg will reappear in the corridor. Don't worry about dropping them, heaving them at the wrong time, or missing your target. Just keep blasting the approaching explosive while the powder keg is in the air and getting closer. It only takes one blow with the magic fist to destroy the explosive. Get into the routine of heaving the powder keg into the air, blasting the explosive missile with one shot, then catching the powder keg. Make sure you're pointed in the right direction to blast the explosive missile.

Catch the powder keg and continue forward. Keep repeating this process until you're close enough to throw the powder keg into the machine.

CAUTION

While you're making tracks back to get another powder keg, be aware that the explosive missiles are going to keep coming.

Aim for the wooden plank bandages on the machine. Watch out for the explosive missiles. They keep coming.

It takes three hits on the wooden plank bandages to destroy the machine.

Ly the fairy is freed by the time you get back to her after destroying the machine.

Ly tells Rayman about Polokus, who might be able to help him get all his powers back. Ly gives Rayman all the power she has.

Then Ly disappears.

Climb the rope ladder.

Turn left and head out to the ledge. Now a purple Lum hangs in the air on the way to the next ledge.

NOTE

Press Ⓑ to grab onto the purple Lums.

The Fairy Glade

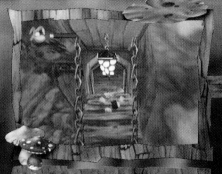

Grab onto the purple Lum and swing over to the other side. Use your chopper ability to glide over to the next ledge.

Leap up between the two columns to climb them.

Walk through the corridor ahead to a pipe. Keep going forward.

Jump off the edge of the pipe and use the chopper ability to glide down and grab the three yellow Lums on the way down.

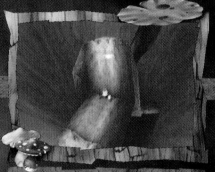

Drop onto the next pipe to get another yellow Lum. Then drop over the side of this pipe as well.

Land on the next pipe down and battle the robo-pirate there for the cage he's guarding. Keep hitting the robo-pirate until he's knocked off. Then break open the cage and take the Lums inside.

Drop down with the chopper ability again and land on the broken bridge below. Walk out through the passageway ahead.

Grab the next yellow Lum.

Murfy approaches you at the next magic stone where the wind funnel is twisting.

TIP

Activate your helicopter in air currents to fly.

Grab the yellow Lum inside the wind funnel.

Maneuver to the next wind funnel. Don't forget to get the yellow Lum at the bottom.

TIP

Let your chopper ability carry you to the top of each wind funnel before you try gliding to the next one.

NOTE

To get the yellow Lum at the bottom here, you'll have to turn off the chopper ability and drop down.

The next wind funnel has another yellow Lum you have to drop down for. Make your way back up the wind funnels.

The next wind funnel has two yellow Lums in it. Go up to get one, then drop down to get the other. Fly back up through the wind funnels.

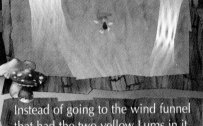

Instead of going to the wind funnel that had the two yellow Lums in it this time, go to the wind funnel to the left.

Grab the yellow Lum inside this wind funnel.

The Fairy Glade

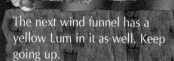

The next wind funnel has a yellow Lum in it as well. Keep going up.

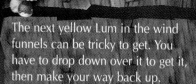

The next yellow Lum in the wind funnels can be tricky to get. You have to drop down over it to get it, then make your way back up.

Shoot the purple Lum ahead to swing out of the wind funnel and swing into the building ahead. Drop through the wind funnel in front of the ledge to collect two more yellow Lums. Make your way back to the purple Lum.

NOTE

It's really easy to miss the two yellow Lums in this wind funnel. Also, you can activate the chopper ability after you get the second yellow Lum so you don't have to fall the entire distance and come back up.

Glide to the ledge.

A Teensie drops out of the cage.

The Teensie opens a warp gate that ends the level. Go through the gate. Back in the Hall of Doors, choose The Marshes of Awakening.

Walk into the little room to the left and look up to spot the pirate cage there. Jump up and blast the cage with your magic fist.

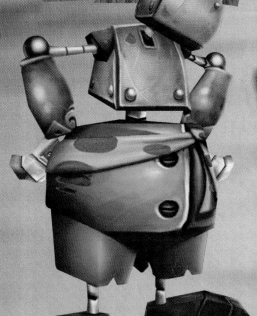

The Marshes of Awakening

Walk down the narrow wooden bridge to get a better look at the marshy countryside.

Note the piranha sign. These are not safe waters!

Turn left and leap out onto the lily pad.

Turn left again and leap onto the nearby tree root. Don't aim for the edge of the root because you slide off too easily.

Follow the tree root around and grab the first yellow Lum waiting ahead. Watch out for the jumping piranha.

Ahead is a dark cave with a ghost guarding the entrance.

NOTE

If you want, you can blow up the ghost with your magic fist.

Run past the ghost and cross the darkness. The tree root continues here even though you can't see it. Inside the cave, a marker on the wall declares: Warning! This is unknown territory. Tourism may be hazardous.

Wow! After a greeting like that, you can't help but be curious. And the guy on the other side of the three bouncing eyeballs looks like just the guy to ask.

Only, this guy definitely isn't the friendly type. To get by him, you're going to have to know the name of this place. But what is that name?

Return to the lily pads.

Leap out onto the first lily pad and make your way around by jumping to the lily pad on the left. The third lily pad offers access to a small lily pad with a red Lum on it. Use your chopper ability to get it safely.

Leap onto the net ahead.

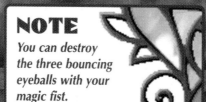

Crawl along the net all the way to the left.

Leap over the top of the net and use your chopper ability to land on the bridge by the green Lum.

Don't leap on the nearby pirate cage—it's a trap and will sink when you land on it.

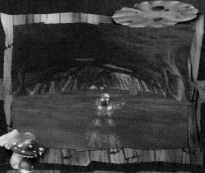

Stand on the bridge and throw your magic fist at the pirate cage to explode it and free Ssssam the Swamp Snake inside.

Ssssam offers to help Rayman get to the other side of the marsh. Shoot the snake's scarf with your magic fist to hang on.

Speed through the swamp, but shoot over the obstacles ahead to grab the red Lums there for extra life. Watch out for piranha.

TIP

Make sure you jump over the submerged rocks. If you try going around them with Rayman on one side and Ssssam on the other, your magic fist rope will break and you'll sink into the water.

Swing out to grab the five yellow Lums on the right wall behind the swinging pendulum blade. They look like part of the torch here.

Look out for the ghosts that rise from the marsh! Weave through them to make it safely.

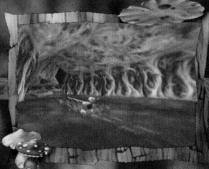

Weave through the crates ahead, too.

Hit the pirate crates half-submerged in the water ahead to get the yellow Lums inside.

NOTE

Don't worry about getting all the Lums and pirate cages the first time through here. It's really hard. Concentrate on finishing the level alive, then you can simply re-enter this area from the Hall of Doors and play again until you get them all. Remember, you have to have all the Lums to qualify for the bonus rounds as well as save the known world.

There are more yellow Lums on the waters as well.

Weave through all the poles sticking up from the water as Ssssam takes you for the ride of your life.

When you ski up onto the bridge to get the yellow Lum there, quickly grab Ssssam's scarf again before the bridge has a chance to completely drop out from under you.

TIP

The yellow Lum on the bridge inside the passageway right after the first explosive is easy to miss. Look for the ramp in the water on the left and take it up. The yellow Lum will be on the bridge on the left side of the passageway.

The Marshes of Awakening

Watch out for the explosive mines.

You have to leap over the first one to get the yellow Lums in the center of them, then ski out wide to miss the explosives.

Other yellow Lums are on top of the poles sticking up from the water. Jump up to get those. The hardest yellow Lum to get is the one hanging at the end of the ghost's fishing pole. You have to avoid his attack, then leap up and grab the Lum.

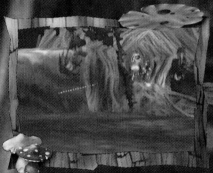

One final leap at the end, and you're on safe ground again.

Break the pirate cage ahead with your magic fist. Grab the green Lum behind you.

Talk to the Teensie you freed to open the warp gate to end this level.

Walk into it and return to the Hall of Doors.

The Walk of Life

Meanwhile, back at the pirate ship, the crew has to deliver bad news to their commander.

Captain Razorbeard isn't happy at all and orders his warships into the area.

A pirate ship dives into the bayou just as Rayman arrives.

Turn left to find a magic stone in a small clearing.

Ly shows up and challenges Rayman to a race.

Follow Ly down the incline and grab all the Lums that you can along the way.

Bounce on the cobwebs and follow Ly.

TIP
Don't use the chopper ability while you bounce through the cobwebs here. It will only slow you down.

Run through the green light ahead and keep collecting Lums.

NOTE
The green lights you run through are time extensions that reset the clock, giving you more time to finish the race.

Bounce across another set of cobwebs and get the Lums on the ledge on the other side.

Follow the line of Lums around to the right.

When you run over the ledge, activate your chopper ability and glide to the bridge. Beware here, though, because the bridge starts falling down behind you!

Keep running and collecting Lums!

Jump onto the climbing vines ahead before the bridge gives out under you.

Head left up the vines.

Race up the bridge.

Drop to the next bridge.

Turn right and dive toward the vines in the cubbyhole. Don't forget the yellow Lum there.

Climb to the top of the ledge and start running again.

Leap out for the next cobweb.

Use the chopper ability to glide out to the webs. As soon as you're over the webs, and you'll know by your shadow, drop the chopper ability.

Bounce to the next ledge.

Follow Ly and grab Lums along the way.

Run to the next ledge.

Leap out and glide to the next ledge where the timer extension is. Grab the yellow Lums along the way.

Turn to the right and leap for the next ledge.

Follow Ly around the ledge and through the cave mouth.

More twists and turns lead to yet another ledge.

Glide to the next ledge with a light on it.

Jump and glide through the next two ledges, left, then right, and grab the Lums along the way.

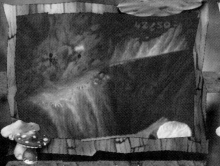

Jump to the next cobweb.

Follow Ly around the ledge and into the next cave.

The Walk of Life

Join Ly at the magic stone to end the race.

Ly gives you some vital energy, then the Teensie appears and opens a warp gate to the Hall of Doors to end this level.

NOTE

Now, if you're incredibly skilled, you may have actually gotten all 50 of the yellow Lums available on this level on the first try. If not, go back through the Walk of Life until you get them all. Remember, you need them all to defeat the robo-pirates and save the world!

RAYMAN 2
THE GREAT ESCAPE

The Bayou

The warships are going to be hunting you on this level, so move quickly. Run and leap onto the barrel ahead. Don't go into the water.

Use your magic fist to detonate the explosives the pirate ships fire at you.

Leap to the ledge to the right before the barrel sinks. Grab the green Lum to save your progress here.

The ledge sticking up in the water has two red Lums on it. Glide over to it and throw your magic fist at the pirate cage.

Grab the two yellow Lums inside the pirate cage.

Leap out onto the next barrel.

Throw your magic fist again to detonate the explosives the pirate ship fires at you.

Leap onto the next ledge where the yellow Lums are inside a tree trunk.

Climb the ladder.

Grab the green Lum at the top of the ladder, then go toward the yellow Lums along the dock.

Get the first yellow Lum, but wait on the second. Throw your magic fist at the switch to the right to lower another bridge.

Grab the second yellow Lum, then glide onto the lowered bridge.

CAUTION

Watch out for the pirate ship that may be in this area!

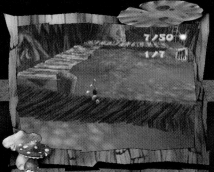

As soon as you land on the lowered bridge, it starts to shake. Run to the left as the bridge falls apart.

You won't be able to run the length of the bridge. Leap into the air and glide over to the next dock.

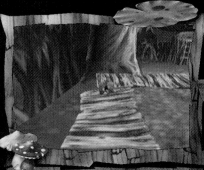

Unfortunately, this dock starts to fall apart as soon as you're on it. Keep running and leap to the next dock!

TIP

The dock structures here actually last longer if you jump along them, touching down every now and then, rather than if you do sustained running. Of course, jumping is a little trickier because you've got a greater chance of dropping into the marsh.

And you'll discover that you're on another rickety structure. Keep running, then leap into the air and glide over to get the three yellow Lums ahead.

Make sure you're gliding, because the robo-pirates shoot out the first section of the final dock before you get there.

Glide to the next section of the dock and run quickly.

Climb the ladder and take the green Lum at the top to save your progress.

Turn right and follow the path through the forest ahead.

Knock out the robo-pirate ahead and break open the cage. A purple Lum flies out.

Chase after the purple Lum. Throw your magic fist at the purple Lum to swing to the next barrel floating in the swamp.

CAUTION

You don't have a lot of time on this purple Lum. It will fade after a few seconds. Make the swing out to the barrel and drop onto it.

Spot the yellow Lum ahead but avoid the ghost.

Walk back and forth across the barrel to collect all the Lums. Leap over the ghosts or shoot them with your magic fist.

Just before the barrel drops over the ledge ahead, jump up and glide to the branch where the two red Lums and the green Lum are.

After you get the Lums, look down to spot a pirate cage. Use your magic fist to break it open.

TIP

You have to move around on the branch to find the right place from which to throw your magic fist.

Don't jump down after the yellow Lum. It will come to you.

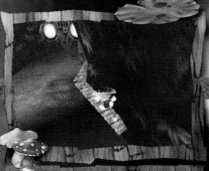

Walk forward, then glide down to get the yellow Lums all in a row here.

Follow the bridge around the corner but be ready. The robo-pirates will shoot the bridge out from under you. Activate your chopper ability and glide to the next section.

The Bayou

Keep running and leaping as the bridge collapses behind you. Grab the yellow Lums ahead and make your way to the small island.

Turn the corner to the right. The bridges ahead are under the warship and a purple Lum hovers off to the left.

Swing onto the purple Lum first.

Drop off onto the tree at the other end and go inside to break the pirate cage there.

TIP

Use the joystick to line up the jump to the tree. Try using this technique with other purple Lum jumps that don't quite line up at first.

Free the yellow Lums inside the pirate cage, but beware of attacks from behind you.

Shoot your magic fist out toward the purple Lum. Adjust your leap off the purple Lum to the bridge that hasn't been blown up by the robo-pirates. Glide down to it.

Go forward and take the next two yellow Lums. Round the bridge and keep going. Take the two yellow Lums there.

The robo-pirates keep firing at you, so streak for the other side. Glide to the tree ahead.

Once you're on the other side, don't enter the tree trunk. Turn around to spot the pirate cage under the bridge.

Break the pirate cage open with your magic fist and get the yellow Lums inside.

Walk into the tree trunk.

Jump up and glide to the log ahead.

Watch out for the piranha as you leap out and take the yellow Lum ahead. Glide over to the right to get the yellow Lums on the gnarled roots.

Continue through the tunnel formed by trees ahead.

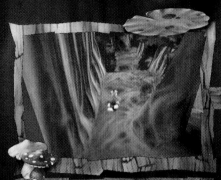

Stay to the left to get some added height for the coming jumps.

Glide over the deadly water below.

Jump and glide again. Turn the corner to face the next robo-pirate here. Shoot him with your magic fist to knock him out.

Use Z to dodge while you're throwing your magic fist.

Ahead is a partial bridge. On a tree trunk to the right is a switch. Use your magic fist to hit the switch.

Cross the extended bridge, but look out for the explosives coming from the trap ahead.

Time the explosives and leap across, without gliding, and grab the green Lum. Run quickly to get through the trap.

TIP

Timing is important with this trap. Wait until the explosive rolls out, then start running. Don't glide. By the time you leap to the other side, you'll be able to grab the green Lum and keep going without getting touched.

The Bayou

Stop quickly after clearing the first trap. Another one is just ahead.

Run and leap the gap. You'll have to time the barrels on the other side as well.

You can even grab onto the ledge's side for a short time if you get hit. Pull up and keep going.

Jump off the explosives without setting them off to gain more height and glide around the bridges to avoid the rolling barrels. Otherwise, you'll have to time them and jump them.

You'll have to jump off the barrels for the greater height if you want to collect the red Lum here.

Leap from the barrel traps to the land ahead. Now that's about enough of that! Whew!

See that yellow Lum? Leap and glide toward it.

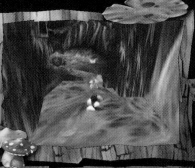

Well, they're still rolling out the barrels ahead. And even faster than before.

You've got to be really fast to get the red Lum here. Jumping over is easy by comparison.

Try aiming for the edge where the barrel rolls across. Wait until the barrel rolls away, then pull yourself up and keep going.

Now there's your worst nightmare!

Plenty of barrel rolling is going on here, and there are yellow Lums to get. Try to get through them quickly. Wait until the barrels start rolling on the ground to make your jumps and keep going.

Hanging onto the ledge while the barrel passes is another good strategy.

Leap and glide into the area ahead.

Grab the green Lum ahead to save your progress.

Turn left to spot the yellow Lum there. This one can be easy to miss. Throw your magic fist at the switch, then scamper back to the bridge.

Line up with the three red Lums on the partial bridge ahead. Now that's some welcome mat!

Walk to the end of the bridge. It can be hard to see, but there's a purple Lum floating out ahead of you.

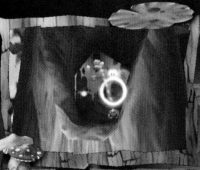

Throw your magic fist at the purple Lum to make the leap into the tree trunk.

Leap over the beast farther back in the tree trunk.

Take a look at the swinging pendulum blades ahead. Looks nasty, doesn't it? And then there's the electrified fence at the other end.

Turn left and shoot your magic fist at the button on the pipe to shut down the electrified fence. This button is on a timer, so run through the swinging pendulum blades quickly.

Avoid the explosive trap in the little room ahead.

Time the barrels and run down the corridor.

The Bayou

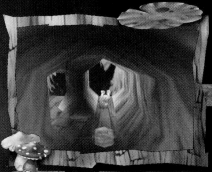

When the barrels catch up with you from behind, leap up to let them pass under.

Turn to the left at the juncture ahead.

Leap on the pipe to get the two yellow Lums here.

As you bounce on the small platforms, spot the pirate cage to the right.

Break the cage open with your magic fist. Leap onto the platforms, following the freed Teensie up the cylinder. Grab the yellow Lums along the way.

Use the chopper ability to better angle your jumps if you need to.

Follow the Teensie at the top to the gate that leads to the Hall of Doors and ends the level.

Don't go through the gate yet. Drop back to the floor where the lowest platforms are. Walk to the ledge overhanging the edge.

Drop onto the ledge and notice the ladder behind you.

Walk forward along the ledge until you spot the final pirate cage you need on this level. Jump up and throw your magic fist to break it open.

The yellow Lum inside comes to you, so you don't have to walk under the falling barrels.

Climb the ladder and bounce back up to the warp gate the Teensie opened. Leap through to go to the Hall of Doors.

The Sanctuary of Water and Ice

Rayman appears in the Council Chamber of the Teensies.

They send Rayman to a totally new world.

Battle the robo-pirate that shows up. Knock him out every time he gets on level ground.

The robo-pirate keeps popping into different places, making him hard to hit.

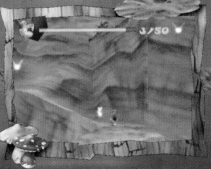

Gather the yellow Lums the robo-pirate is defending.

Keep crowding the robo-pirate up the ledges and blast him away. Grab the two red Lums he gives you.

TIP

Don't get frustrated at the lone crab wandering the beachfront. You can't kill it no matter how hard you try, but he can sure put the hurt on you.

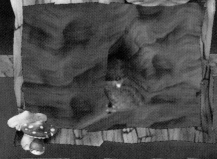

Once the robo-pirate is gone and you climb to the top of the ledges to gather all the yellow Lums, you're able to see a small crack in the stone wall that leads to more yellow Lums. Don't go there yet.

Turn around and use the first-person view (©▲) to scan the beach. A pirate cage hangs at the end of the narrow dock.

Go break the pirate cage open to free the yellow Lums inside, but beware of the crab guarding the dock. If you fall in the water you'll die.

NOTE

Make sure you get all the yellow Lums out of this cage. Jump up if you have to. It's easy to miss a few if you're busy dodging the crab!

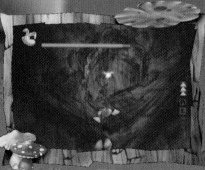

Return to the ledges and go through the crack in the stone wall.

Get the green Lum in the water to save your place.

Then dive down and get the yellow Lums underwater.

Find the tunnel by the big flower and follow it through to get the Lums inside.

At the other end of the tunnel, find a pirate cage in a small, underwater cave. Break it open and free the Lums, then swim back through the tunnel.

Hop out onto the ledge by the crates. Get the yellow Lum by the rope ladder and climb the ladder.

Take all the yellow Lums near the rope ladder as you climb.

At the top, drop over the ledge and take the green Lum to save your place.

Piranha-infested waters lie ahead. Take the steps to the left.

The next beach has more buildings.

And there are more robo-pirates that burrow up from the sand!

After you knock out the robo-pirates, avoid the crab and try to enter the building on the left. Read the nearby sign: Free dumping for anyone who can figure out how to open the door.

The door to the other building on the right doesn't open either.

Grab the Lums to the right.

Follow the ledge here on around to find a powder keg. Now, *that's* a door opener!

Go back around the corner and blast open the door there first.

Enter the doorway and follow the steps up.

Murfy shows up to tell you about the magic sphere.

TIP

Here's a magic sphere. To grab it, stand in front of it. If you want to toss it in the air, press Ⓐ. Put the spheres onto bases of the same color and the temple doors will open. If you lose a sphere, return to the place where you first took it. You'll find it there.

Walk up the steps and take the magic sphere. Return to the beach.

Throw the magic sphere on the nearest triangular base. It immediately falls into place.

Go back and get another powder keg. Go to the other locked door. You've figured out how to open it, right?

The Sanctuary of Water and Ice

Poof! No more door. Enter and follow the ramp up.

Another magic sphere lies ahead.

Take this magic sphere back out to the beach and throw it onto the other base.

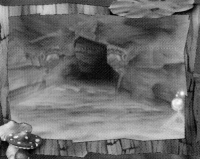

With both magic spheres in place, the temple doors open.

Enter the temple. Follow the corridor to another green Lum.

Look all around this big room to find the yellow Lums here.

Walk through the doorway filled with stars.

The next place you arrive doesn't look like it'll be a good time at all.

Walk through the doors ahead and get ready to slide down the ramp from side to side to collect the yellow Lums.

NOTE

To get all the yellow Lums here, you're going to have to be incredibly lucky or skilled. Otherwise, choose to die a number of times in the cracks between the jumps. You'll probably have to come back through this area more than once to get them all. Pulling back on the joystick slows your downhill run somewhat, as does running up against the railings and staying there. This gives you a little control over where you're going and how fast. However, sometimes you need that speed build-up to get across a particularly wide jump. Jumping also gives you a little control, but not much. Choose to die before you go through the door at the end, then keep coming back, remembering where the yellow Lums are and making the necessary changes to get them all. It takes some time, but it can be done.

Make the big jump at the end.

Continue sliding and grab the yellow Lums along the way.

More yellow Lums lie ahead.

Another door opens up ahead.

In mere seconds, you're face-to-face with Axel, guardian of the sanctuary.

Dodge Axel's thrown icicles and shoot the purple Lum with your magic fist.

Swing over to the other ledge and shoot the next purple Lum.

NOTE

Shooting the purple Lums while on the move dodging Axel can be tough. Stick with it and get a pattern going. Remember to turn loose of the first purple Lum by pressing Ⓐ, then quickly shoot your magic fist out by pressing Ⓑ. Wait until you're at the top of the swinging arc each time to let go of the last purple Lum. Then hit the Ⓐ and Ⓑ in rapid succession to make the next swing.

When you get to the other end of the swings, shoot the stalactite to drop it on Axel and knock him out.

When Axel disappears, a single purple Lum floats out.

The purple Lum floats into position in front of you.

Swing to the cave at the end of the line of purple Lums.

NOTE

Now that Axel is gone, take time with your swings. Swing back and forth until you're sure you're lined up with the next purple Lum, then shoot your magic fist out and go.

The Sanctuary of Water and Ice

Use the chopper ability to leap off the purple Lum and land safely in the running water.

Don't enter the cave yet. Turn and walk to the side, following the ledge around the outside of the building.

Walk behind the building to get the red Lums and the yellow Lum.

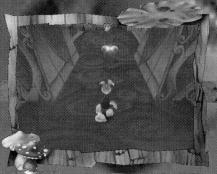

Now enter the front opening and walk straight up to collect the Lums along the way.

Walk up the long ramp ahead.

Your powers automatically activate the altar ahead.

When the altar shifts, grab the first mask of Polokus.

You're instantly transported to another place. Polokus sits on an altar before you.

Polokus awakens and tells you that he will help you once the three other masks are brought to him.

He fits the mask into place.

Then Polokus uses his magic to send Rayman back to the Hall of Doors to end the level.

The Menhir Hills

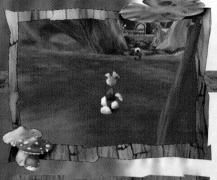

As soon as you dive through the opening in the Hall of Doors, you can easily see you've arrived in a strange and wondrous land.

Murfy shows up long enough to warn you that a walking shell guards the place. He also says he's heard it was possible to tame it. Watch out—here it comes now!

Before the walking shell reaches you, turn and run behind the big tree with the vortex to the Hall of Worlds. A smaller tree there has a switch. Throw a magic fist at it.

Head over to these three trees to the left of the switch. See that square hole? There was a grate here like the one in the Fairy Glade. Well, don't just stand there; jump in!

When you've got your feet back, follow the tunnel to this pirate cage suspended above the water. Release five yellow Lums from their prison. Return to where you landed when you fell down here.

Take a look up to see the cobwebs clinging to the wall. Climb them to return to the grassy glade above. The walking shell will still be there and looking for you.

Run away from the walking shell to exhaust it.

When the walking shell lines up behind you, leap up into the air and land on its back to ride it like a horse.

Use the joystick to control the walking shell's direction. Ride it across the lava.

RAYMAN 2
THE GREAT ESCAPE

NOTE

Mounting the walking shell can be difficult. Running away from it and waiting for it to exhaust itself seems to be the most consistent way to mount it. Another way is to leap three or four times, always away from the walking shell, until you land on it after it gives out. Also, if you run too far ahead of it, it will return to where it started. Stay just ahead of it until it tuckers out.

Ride the walking shell close enough to the door straight ahead that it can't change directions. Then hop off and watch it explode the door.

Step inside the blown-up door and break the pirate cage inside to free the Lums trapped there.

Leap over the railing to the left. This is a military academy.

Enter the door.

Approach the next room slowly. Get the green Lum to save your place.

Stay to the right side of the room to avoid waking the sleeping robo-pirates.

TIP

As long as you move slowly in this room, you won't make enough noise to wake the robo-pirates.

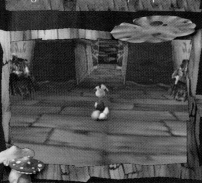

In the middle of the room, turn and face the door the sleeping robo-pirates are guarding.

Walk quietly and carefully between the robo-pirates and you won't wake them. You'll be able to enter the door at the end of the hallway.

TIP

If you wake the robo-pirates by accident, run outside to reset this game sequence. The room they're guarding contains a pirate cage that you definitely need. Just keep a light finger on the joystick.

Inside the room, turn left to find the pirate cage containing yellow Lums.

Use your magic fist to break open the cage. Quietly walk back down the hallway past the robo-pirates and turn left.

Walk through the door and follow the hallway to the left.

There's definitely a lot that needs to be done in this area.

Look to the right and you'll spot another walking shell in its house.

Ignore the walking shell for the moment and approach the mushroom.

Jump on the mushroom to get up to the next mushroom in the tree.

Throw your magic fist at the purple Lum hanging here.

Swing out as far as you can and use your chopper ability to glide over to the house.

TIP

After playing against Axel in the last level, you've probably got a hair-trigger finger. If you use the chopper ability too soon, you won't get enough arc to glide over to your target building. Wait just a moment before you use the glide ability, otherwise you'll end up short.

Grab the yellow Lum in the corner.

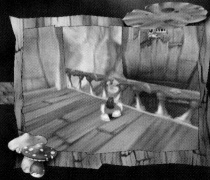

Turn right and spot the pirate cage hanging from the next building.

The Menhir Hills

Jump up and throw your magic fist to break the cage. Wait for the Lums to come to you.

Drop back into the yard.

Approach the walking shell, then run around the tree until it gives up. You'll collect the yellow Lum behind it at the same time.

Mount up, cowboy!

Ride the walking shell through the tunnel ahead. Jockey from side to side to gather all the yellow Lums, and watch out for the thorn vine that erupts from the ground.

Keep riding out onto the dock, but avoid the crates.

TIP

There is an alternate dock here, but it ends up in the same cave. However there are red Lums here to grab if you're skilled enough.

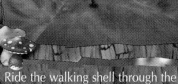

Ride through the door ahead and enter another cave with thorn vines that shoot up from the ground unexpectedly.

Grab all the yellow Lums along the way.

Ride the walking shell close enough to the door ahead to explode it, but jump off before you get there!

Don't enter the door yet. That can wait. Turn left and walk toward the tower.

Turn and face the building. A powder keg is on the right and a door is on the left on the bottom story.

TIP

If you hop off the walking shell too early and it doesn't explode the door, use the powder keg here.

Now go through the door that the walking shell blasted open. Grab the yellow Lum inside.

Follow the corridor and quietly walk up on the sleeping robo-pirate ahead.

Check out the skull-faced door. Turn left and keep following the ledge.

Use your magic fist on the switch ahead.

Go quietly back to the door and go inside.

NOTE

OK, if you really want to blow up the sleeping robo-pirate, you can use your magic fist or you can pack a powder keg up here and throw it at him.

The room is filled with smashed robo-pirate parts.

Another friend of yours, Clark, is there, too, really looking worse for the wear. After a quick conversation, you learn that he swallowed something bad for him and needs some life potion. The potion is hidden near the entrance to the Marshes of Awakening in a place called the Cave of Bad Dreams.

NOTE

As you'll recall, this is the cave you couldn't enter earlier. Now that you know the name, you can.

Rayman takes off, ending up back at the Hall of Doors. Go to the Marshes of Awakening and enter.

The Cave of Bad Dreams

Walk out to the end of the dock and leap onto the lily pad.

Jump to the log on the left next.

Walk up the log and enter the cave at the end.

Walk past the bouncing eyeballs to talk to the guy there.

The old man sends Rayman through a warp, promising a race. A prize is there to be won, but the old man will show Rayman no mercy if he catches him!

Once the trail opens before you, start running!

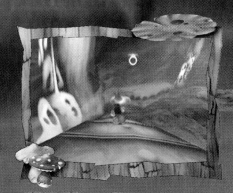

Use the purple Lum to swing over to the next section of the path.

Glide down to the next ledge.

Leap and glide to the ledge to the right to grab the green Lum there to save your place.

Leap and glide to the skull islands in the middle of the water. Move quickly because they sink under you.

Glide to the wall of bones where the red Lums are. Climb up.

After gathering the Lums, leap out and glide to the next series of skull islands. You have to hurry because the skull islands sink shortly after they drop into the water!

TIP

One of the best things to do if you're having problems with this set of skull islands is to hold onto the wall and wait. A second set of skull islands will drop from the ceiling after the first set sinks. Jump out and start gliding toward the falling second set of islands here and hurry across. To save time, stop using the chopper ability as soon as you're sure you're over an island.

Jump onto the blocks ahead.

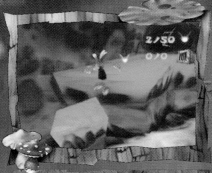

Keep going forward and grab the Lums ahead.

Watch out for the creepy arm that sticks out of the cave to swipe at you!

Shoot the purple Lum ahead to swing across the water.

Glide over to the bone wall and climb up to the yellow Lum.

Drop onto the ledge to the left.

Turn left and grab the yellow Lum at the other end.

The Cave of Bad Dreams

Glide over to the bone column sticking up from the water. Start climbing at once before the column starts sinking.

TIP
Don't just climb the bone column, jump to gain extra yardage up the column.

Run to the other side of the bone column, leap off, and fire your magic fist to catch the purple Lum.

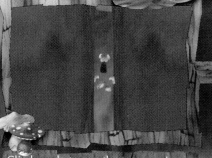

Leap from the second bone column to the third one. Make sure you run across the top.

Glide to the next ledge.

Take the green Lum ahead, then follow the tunnel. Grab the yellow Lums along the way and watch out for the grasping skeletal arms that pop from the walls.

Climb up between the two moving columns and grab the ledge above. Don't worry about the yellow Lum behind you. You'll get it in a moment.

Turn around and glide down to get the yellow Lum you left behind.

Climb back up the columns to the ledge. Take the two red Lums on either side of the ledge here.

Walk to the right side of the ledge and look down at the crabs and ledges below.

Glide down. Avoid the crabs and grab the yellow Lums on this ledge.

Blast the fire-throwing crabs over the ledge.

Take the magic sphere they leave behind.

Throw the magic sphere on top of the triangular base.

The magic sphere and base raise up to reveal a hole in the ledge. Go through the hole.

Drop down and get the green Lum. Turn around to get the yellow Lum behind you.

Avoid the caterpillars in the next cavern and leap up the ledge on the left.

Follow the ledge until you reach the cave on the left.

Enter the cave.

Take the green Lum to save your place here, then go through the tunnel on the left. Leave the one on the right for later.

Glide across the skull islands.

When the second skull island pops up from the water, leap to the twisting stone bridge above when it turns toward you.

Pull yourself up onto the twisting bridge.

Leap and glide to the ledge where the two yellow Lums and red Lum are. Then leap back onto the spinning bridge.

The Cave of Bad Dreams

Leap to the single red Lum next.

Leap and glide onto the next spinning bridge.

Leap and glide from the spinning bridge to the ledge with the green Lum and the magic sphere.

Throw the magic sphere out onto the spinning bridge. Wait until the bridge comes around again, then leap out after it.

TIP

Don't worry about missing with the magic sphere—it's magic! If it falls down into the water, it will reappear in your hands back on the last ledge you were on!

Throw the magic sphere to the next ledge, then the second bridge after that. Keep throwing it until you get it back to the cave entrance where you came in.

Leap and glide down to the magic sphere.

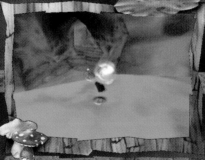

Take the magic sphere back to the main cavern where the caterpillars are.

Throw the magic sphere onto its matching base. There's one more to find.

Return to the cave and take the tunnel on the right this time.

Throw your magic fist at the purple Lum overhead and swing over to the next ledge.

Leap onto the moving skull and take a ride over to the next ledge. Grab the red Lum there.

Follow the ledge to grab another red Lum and the yellow Lum.

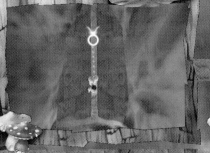

Shoot your magic fist at the purple Lum and swing out.

Wait until the big doors open, then leap out from the purple Lum and glide into the next cavern. Land on the ledge where the green Lum is.

TIP

It doesn't really matter if the doors are open or closed. You can get through if you swing off straight. It just seems easier when they're open. Also, if you fall short on your jump, you can climb between the closed doors to get additional height. Don't give up there. You can still make it.

Leap and glide to the next column, then take the moving skull platform.

Use your magic fist on all the caterpillars in the next area. Jump to all the platforms ahead to get the yellow Lums there.

Hop on the next skull island to get lifted to the level above.

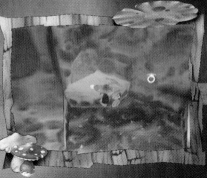

Take the green Lum and the magic sphere you find there.

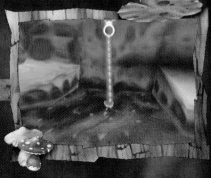

Throw the magic sphere to the next ledge.

From the next ledge, throw the magic sphere to the ledge you entered on. It's to the left of the purple Lum.

Glide out toward the purple Lum.

Shoot your magic fist at the purple Lum to grab hold.

The Cave of Bad Dreams

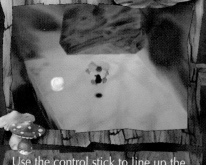

Use the control stick to line up the jump and glide that you need to make to join the magic sphere.

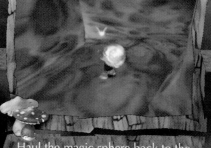

Haul the magic sphere back to the main cavern.

Throw the magic sphere onto the pedestal to reveal the secret door to the left.

Go inside the cavern and grab the yellow and red Lums waiting on you.

Throw your magic fist into the green crystals sticking up from the ground to reveal another hole.

Drop through the hole in the ground. Break the crystals sticking up from the ground ahead with your magic fist to go through.

The scary old man climbs up from the green water.

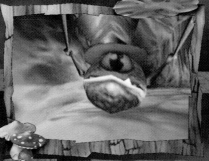

And he's come to eat you up if you're too slow! Get moving!

The old man is hot on your tail as you glide down the sloping cavern. Grab the Lums along the way.

NOTE

You have choices to make on your downhill run. Sometimes you have to go for Lums in hard-to-get-to spots. Other times you have to use your magic fist to break the crystals ahead.

By the time you finish this downhill run, you should have 45 of the yellow Lums. There are four five-packs along the way.

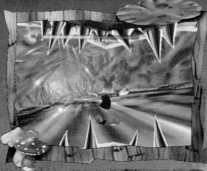

Keep shooting your magic fist to break the crystals ahead.

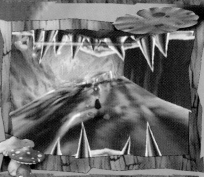

Don't forget you've got to get all the yellow Lums on this level!

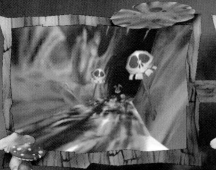

In the end, it looks like you've made your escape.

But the scary man is already waiting for you with breath that'll set you on fire!

Throw your magic fist at him.

When he puts up the skulls as a barrier, shoot them with your magic fist to freeze them in place.

NOTE

Shooting the skulls is going to take some work. Your reflexes and muscle memory are going to have to be trained through some repetition. The strategy here is to shoot a skull close enough to you that you can jump on it. Wait for the next skull, then shoot it and jump again. Usually it takes three skulls to make it completely across the chasms. It's not easy, but it can be done with some patience and some willingness to learn by doing.

Your objective here is to make a bridge to get to the scary man.

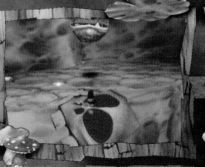

Jump from the last skull to reach the green Lum here as well as the red ones.

Turn back around and chase after your target again.

Your quarry immediately turns tail and runs to the next ledge. Now that you've learned the necessary skills, go after him again by building another bridge.

On the next ledge, throw your magic fist out to a purple Lum. Make sure you're not hit by a fireball as you swing out or you'll fall to your death.

TIP

Run all the way to the left, then cut back across to the right and throw the magic fist at the purple Lum while you're on the run.

The Cave of Bad Dreams

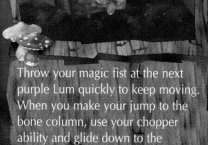

Throw your magic fist at the next purple Lum quickly to keep moving. When you make your jump to the bone column, use your chopper ability and glide down to the bottom to get the red Lums there.

Climb the bone column and get ready to dodge fireballs.

On the bone column, watch as your quarry retreats. Then freeze more skulls into place to make a bridge. Leap over to the next ledge.

Glide over to the column to the right to get more yellow Lums.

Keep jumping from column to column, taking the red Lums along the way.

TIP

When you have to stop the skulls here, try shooting the second one before leaping onto the first one. Also, the skulls come more quickly, so get them closer together and try not to glide to save time.

TIP

Once you get to this column, some of the pressure goes away. You may die, but the two red Lums that keep coming back on this column will keep you alive if you remember to get them each time. Just work on your timing. The best thing you can do is shoot, jump, shoot, and jump again. Don't look to see if your shot actually stopped the skull, because that will eat away at your time. You've got the red Lum health backing you up, so trust yourself and the auto-aiming on your fist and go for it!

Make another bridge of skulls and jump over to the column where the green Lum is to save your place.

CAUTION

If you stand too close to the edge, sometimes the skull teeth whip around and knock you off when you hit a skull with the magic fist. Sometimes when they impact against the column they'll knock you off if you're too close to the edge. Give yourself some room to work. Also, you have to move to the front of the skull in order to shoot the next one consistently.

When you get four skulls in a row, you get a small breather while waiting for the next skull. Don't panic. Just wait for the next skull.

Shoot and jump fast to keep going until you reach the ledge.

Spot the skull in the back on the right and walk toward it.

Follow the trail.

Wow! Look at all that gold!

A single coin rolls at your feet.

You're offered the treasure by the scary man. It's in your best interests to turn it down.

After you turn the treasure down, you're warped out of the treasure room.

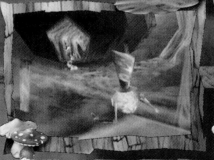

You're given the Elixir of Life, and that sounds like something Clark could really use right now.

Run back along the tree root.

Leap to the lily pad.

Leap to the dock and enter the Teensie warp gate to return to the Hall of Doors.

The Cave of Bad Dreams

Return to the Menhir Hills

Back in the Menhir Hills, get the walking shell tired out and mount up.

Ride the walking shell into the door again, but jump off before you get there.

Creep back into the military academy.

Go slowly through the room with the sleeping robo-pirates again.

Get back on the walking shell in the yard and take it for a ride.

Ride through the tunnel and back across the dock.

Ride through the next tunnel and get off before you hit the door ahead. Enter.

Tiptoe by the robo-pirate and throw your magic fist at the switch. Enter the door quietly.

Give the Elixir to Clark and he feels better immediately.

Clark gets up and knocks a hole in the wall.

Follow Clark through the hole.

Turn right and follow the corridor with Clark guarding your back.

A gate blocks the way ahead.

A purple Lum also hovers near the ceiling above.

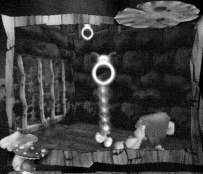

Swing from one purple Lum to the next higher one.

Spot the third purple Lum even higher.

Throw your magic fist into the fourth purple Lum above and swing up to spot the pirate cage there.

Glide over to the ledge where the pirate cage is and break it open with your magic fist.

Grab the yellow Lums inside the pirate cage.

Drop back down to the third purple Lum and swing around to spot the ledge on the wall. Glide over to the ledge.

Go through the doorway.

Flip the red switch to let Clark out of the other room.

Once Clark joins you in the hallway, walk down the corridor.

A gate blocks the way at the end of the corridor.

Kind of looks like a dead end, doesn't it? It's a good thing Clark punches another hole in the wall here.

Follow Clark through the hole and spot the stairs leading down in the middle of the floor. Take the stairs to reach the great outdoors.

As you look around this next area, you can see there's a lot to do. Ahead and above across the way is another pirate cage by a purple Lum.

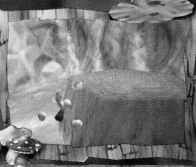

Hop up on the nearby stump.

Leap up and shoot the purple Lum. Swing up and glide over to the pirate cage.

Pull up on the ledge and blast the cage open.

Drop down to the ground and lure the walking shell into the open. Run around until you exhaust the walking shell.

Once the walking shell is exhausted, enter the cave it came out of.

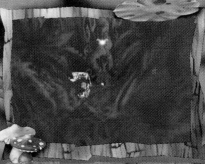

Grab the yellow Lum there and climb the vine.

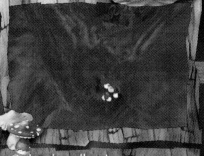

Leap off the vine and activate your chopper ability. Throw your magic fist until the pirate cage there breaks.

Gather the yellow Lums once they're freed. You'll have to climb up the vine again.

Drop down and turn left to enter the tunnel there. The walking shell will follow you. Run up the hill inside the tunnel until the walking shell gives out.

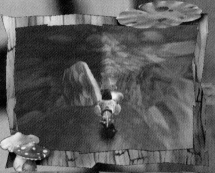

Hop on the walking shell and ride up the hill. Grab the yellow Lums along the way.

Dodge the root tentacles that erupt from the ground.

NOTE

Riding the walking shell across this section is tough. It's going to take some patience and repetition. Just work with it and pay attention to memorizing the route.

Even more rocks and yellow Lums are ahead.

Ride across the dock ahead and grab the yellow Lums along the way.

In a short time, you're blasting through another tunnel after dodging the rocks along the dock.

You come out on the other side of the cave. The walking shell takes you to the warp gate to end the level.

Return to the Menhir Hills

Walk forward in the cave, then throw your magic fist at the spider that drops down on you until it goes away.

TIP

When the spider shows up, immediately retreat to the back of the cave here. If you let the spider chase you forward, you'll fall over the ledge and die most of the time. Don't try to climb the webs outside to get away, either. It is a spider after all. Pay attention to the spider. Landing a shot makes it go transparent for a few seconds. Your shots will pass right through it until it becomes solid again. This spider is very tough to kill. Hang in there.

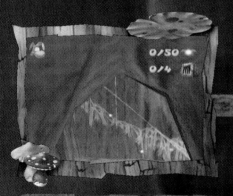

Walk toward the webs at the other end of this corridor.

At the ledge, crawl along the cobweb to gather the yellow Lums.

Go down low to gather all the yellow Lums there.

Jump up to grab the next cobweb and work your way around it.

Only a short distance away, you'll find a pirate cage filled with trapped yellow Lums.

Land on the ledge and use your magic fist to break the cage open. Wait until the Lums come to you.

TIP

It can be a little difficult to hit the pirate cage from the ledge. Walk around and experiment with different positions and you'll get it. Usually, standing closest to the ledge does the job.

TIP

Be sure to notice the purple Lum out in the center of the cobwebs. If you happen to fall anywhere along the way, remember to shoot your magic fist out there to try to catch yourself.

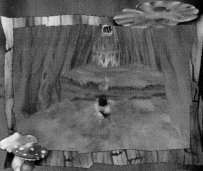

Turn around and walk into the cavern mouth to spot the next pirate cage hanging there.

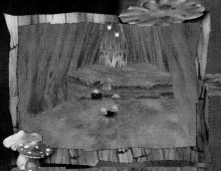

Stay on this ledge and break the pirate cage open.

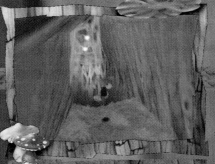

Leap and glide across the chasm in front of you.

Glide over the next chasm as well. Climb up the cobweb to the ledge to get the freed yellow Lums.

Go down the next hole in front of you.

Leap across the mushrooms.

On the ground, take the plank bridge to the left.

Blast the robo-pirate ahead to get him out of the way.

To get this elusive little yellow Lum, leap at it at an angle, then use the chopper ability to glide back to the plank.

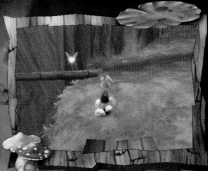

After you read the notice about public enemy two posted by the robo-pirates, return across the planks. Walk across the next plank bridge to the left.

The Canopy

As you try to enter the cave ahead, an electrified security gate closes. Get the yellow Lum here. Walk back across the plank.

Walk back across the first plank.

Walk to the plank to the right and stop at the end. Throw your magic fist to hit the switch to the left of the lock-up gate and release Globox.

Globox is happy to be free again. However, you're not exactly out of trouble here.

Walk back to the security gate and you'll find Globox has joined you there. However, the security gate still closes.

Walk closer and Globox will do his infamous rain dance and short out the electrified bars.

Enter the doorway and leap over the ledge. Use your chopper ability and make sure you get the yellow Lum.

Walk forward to grab the green Lum there.

Turn right to spot the yellow Lum in hiding.

Grab the two yellow Lums by the plant. Scout around the ledge to grab the other yellow Lum here.

Watch as Globox performs another rain dance to make the plant swell and throw out a pink flower blossom.

Hop onto the pink flower and jump again quickly to get the yellow Lum above it.

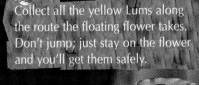

TIP

Don't worry if you fall off the flower. It will come back.

Collect all the yellow Lums along the route the floating flower takes. Don't jump; just stay on the flower and you'll get them safely.

Leap off onto the ledge on the other side and collect the yellow Lums there.

Walk along the ledge and enter the cave on the left.

Boy, look at that fire ahead. You could really use Globox and his rain dance here, huh?

Go to the pillar outside and spot the wooden plank bandages on it. Blast the top of the pillar off with your magic fist.

The broken end lands on the last ledge so Globox can walk along it to join you.

Walk toward the cave with the fire and Globox will follow you.

Inside the cave, Globox will do his rain dance again.

When the fire goes out, cross the ledge and grab the green Lum.

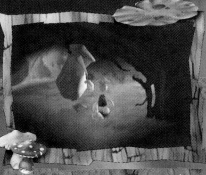

In the next cave you're going to be attacked immediately. Get moving!

Blast the robo-pirate in front of you with your magic fist.

The Canopy

Globox becomes very afraid.

Rayman wishes he had more of his power.

Globox reaches down his throat to get more silver Lums. They make Rayman's fist even stronger.

TIP
To make Rayman's magic fist stronger, hold Ⓑ down longer.

Ahead and around the corner, another pirate ship appears, Globox runs and hides.

Dodge the pirate ship's cannon attack.

When the pirate ship flies away, look out for the robo-pirates left behind.

Hold Ⓑ down to throw your stronger magic fist and blast the robo-pirate.

Gather the red Lum to the right.

Another security gate seals up the next cave containing another green Lum.

Turn around and walk back to find Globox.

When you've got Globox, have him do another rain dance to short out the security gate.

Grab the green Lum and follow the corridor around to get more yellow Lums.

Battle the robo-pirate around the next turn and put it down.

Keep following the corridor to the next big cave.

Look up to spot the pirate cage hanging there. Also notice the wings on the other side of the ridge ahead.

Collect the yellow Lums on the other side of the ridge first.

Climb the crates.

Turn right and look up at the railing around the top of the building. There's a five-pack of yellow Lums there.

Jump up and shoot your magic fist at the purple Lum to the left of the railing.

Swing over to the crate. Hop off the purple Lum and use your chopper ability. Fire your magic fist at the cage to break it. It may take a couple of climbing trips up the crates to accomplish this.

Climb the crates and shoot your magic fist at the purple Lum again. Use the joystick to turn around and leap toward the railing by the five-pack of yellow Lums.

TIP

You know that little open place behind the boxes that looks like you could just fall right on over? Well, you can. So watch it!

Go back and get Globox to follow you into the big cavern.

The Canopy

Walk to the door, but stay out of the red light or the door will shut. However, that's hard to do. The doors close every time.

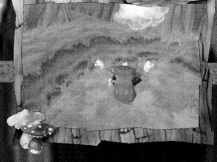

Watch as Globox does his rain dance once more. The purple flower grows huge.

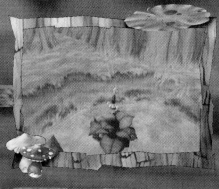

Hide yourself in the purple plant.

This time the ID scan passes you through the door.

Go on down the corridor.

Leap out of the bush and turn the corner to find the last pirate cage.

Break open the pirate cage with your magic fist to free the Teensie and the yellow Lums inside.

Take the warp gate to finish this level. Back in the Hall of Doors, Whale Bay opens up. Go to it and jump in.

Whale Bay

Walk up the steps ahead.

To the right is a fish tank.

Go through the passageway on the left for the moment.

Ahead is a barrel-shaped robo-pirate that is extremely tough.

Even if you take your lumps and run around the barrel-shaped guard, the exit is electrified. Notice the other fish tank in this room. Lucky for you there's a way around him.

TIP

Can't stand the thought of walking away and leaving an enemy unscathed? It can be tough. But the barrel-shaped guard here is hard to beat. However, there is a strategy: by now you've noticed that your magic fist bounces off walls for awhile. Line up in the corridor, then bounce your magic fist into the walls to make a ricochet shot that gives the barrel-shaped guard no chance at all of returning fire. Just remember that if you don't go into the water, you won't find the yellow Lum that's there.

There's even a nifty little switch on the wall by this fish tank. Too bad it's impossible to hit from here.

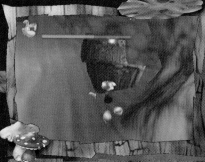

Go back to the first fish tank in the other room.

Dive into the fish tank and swim down.

Take the blue air Lums and red health Lums as you need them and keep swimming with the wall to your left.

Grab the yellow Lum from the treasure chest.

Turn left over the treasure chest to spot the sunken crates.

Follow the trail of sunken crates up to the surface.

Surface in the next tank. As you look around, you'll discover this is the room with the red switch.

Throw your magic fist into the switch.

Hop out of the tank and spot the barrel-shaped robo-pirate ahead.

Turn right and discover the doorway is no longer electrified.

Grab the green Lum on the net. Turn right and walk down to the end of the net.

Hop over the end of the net and to the beam below.

Leap up from the bottom beam and grab the net. Climb along the net to grab the red Lums underneath. Watch out for the leaping piranha.

NOTE

The red Lums under the net are on a timer, so you have to move fast and dodge the leaping piranha. You can still fire your magic fist if you want.

Return to the beam and follow it around to the right.

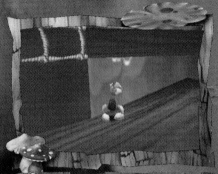

A short distance ahead, you'll find another net with four yellow Lums hanging under it.

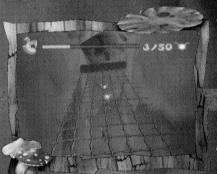

Climb along the net, grab the yellow Lums, and dodge the piranha.

Return to the beam and cross over the top of the net.

Grab the green Lum around the corner and look out at the pirate ship below.

Jump over the railing.

NOTE

Don't worry about the robo-pirate firing at you. His shots are easy to avoid as you make a dash for the railing. He does keep jumping around the ship. If he lands near you while you're on the ship, just do your best to hammer him and avoid his shots. Then get off the ship as soon as you can.

Once you're on the ground, you'll spot a guarded door and a barrel by the ship.

Return to the barrel and turn around to find a red Lum up against the wall. Jump up on the barrel near the boat.

Leap onto the net in front of you and climb up.

Whale Bay

Turn around and look up by the
doorway you glided through to spot
the switch. Hit it with your magic fist.

Glide over to the ship's deck
through the doorway.

Turn around and look up by the
doorway you glided through to spot
the switch. Hit it with your magic fist.

The electrified area vanishes from
the door.

Jump down and go through the
doorway. Watch out for the
exploding barrels ahead.

Time the barrels, then dart around the
corner and jump across the barrels to
get the yellow Lums there. Your chopper ability really comes in handy here.

TIP

*Don't linger in the short hallway
once you enter the door. That robo-
pirate on the deck has you in his
sights now. He'll blast you from
behind if you don't get moving.*

Turn the corner to the right.

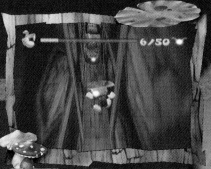

Ahead is a sleeping robo-pirate.

Drop into the water below.

Turn around and grab the red Lum
under the dock you walked off of.

Keep the wall to the right and walk
slowly forward until you reach a
cave with a powder keg in it.

Take the powder keg and go sing the
robo-pirate a final lullaby-bye!

Grab the red Lum in the treetop.

Go back for another powder keg. Try to blow the door open ahead. There's another pirate cage on the other side of this door holding five yellow Lums and a purple Lum. The explosion releases them all from the cage. Watch the purple Lum float up into the air.

NOTE

Sometimes this explosion blows the door, sometimes not. If the powder keg goes through the door and explodes, you won't ever see the cage. The Lums will still fly out even with the door intact.

Climb up through the trees to reach the purple Lum.

Shoot the purple Lum with your magic fist.

Change directions with the joystick. Then leap off and glide into the building ahead.

Follow the corridor and down the next dock.

Walk to the magic stone on the beach. Murfy shows back up and tells you Carmen the whale is trapped. The robo-pirates are going to use her to make oil for the prison ship.

Dive into the water.

Don't swim away from the beach. Dive straight down and turn back toward the beach to find Carmen caged underwater here, but be careful of the electric fence holding her in.

To the left of Carmen's cage is a hole in the wall.

Swim through the hole in the wall.

Whale Bay

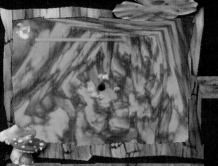

Follow the line of blue Lums.

Swim up through the rectangular opening ahead to surface.

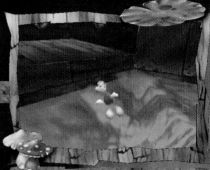

Swim to the low side of the opening and jump out.

Look back over the rectangular opening to spot the opening to the left.

Leap over and grab the ledge. Pull yourself up.

Walk up the passageway to find a door blocking your way.

Return to the end of the corridor overlooking the rectangular area. Two doorways lie ahead.

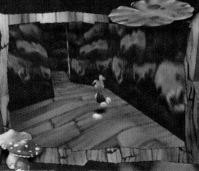

Take the doorway to the right.

Turn right and look down into the room below. Those stairs definitely look interesting. However, there's still another door back around the rectangular pool area. Return there.

Turn right and leap into the doorway there that you haven't tried yet.

Follow the corridor around and collect the yellow Lums along the way.

In just a moment you're in the room you looked down into with the interesting steps.

Walk up the steps.

Spot the switch on the opposite wall.

Look down into the water to spot Carmen trapped below.

Throw your magic fist at the switch. Once the electrified field drops away, Carmen wastes no time in getting out.

The electrical machinery on the wall transports a walking shell into the room. Run around to wear it out.

Mount up, cowboy!

Ride the walking shell into the corridor opposite the steps. You're going to ride it to the locked door you found earlier.

TIP

If you die and have to come back to this area, you have to activate the red switch that freed Carmen again to activate the transporter and bring the walking shell into the room.

Ride the walking shell through the curving corridor.

Press Ⓑ to boost the walking shell's speed and get across the water.

Hop off the walking shell before it hits the door.

Walk through the door and follow the corridor around to more red Lums.

Whale Bay

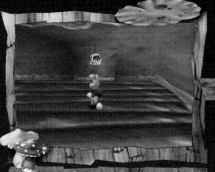

At the top of the steps is another pirate cage.

Blast the cage open and take the yellow Lums inside.

Turn left and follow the corridor.

Walk out onto the ramp and stop at the end.

Below, bubbles glow in the water.

Dive into the water and swim. The line of bubbles leads you to Carmen. These are air bubbles Carmen is leaving for you.

TIP

You have to swim through the air bubbles Carmen leaves to get the extra air she's leaving for you. The air bubbles are also on timers, so you have to hurry to get them before they fade away.

Trail Carmen into an underground cave.

Keep following Carmen.

In a short time, Carmen leads you to a brand new cavern.

In this new room, you have to watch out for the piranhas swimming around. They'll take the air bubbles. Stay close to Carmen.

Swim through the light streamers cutting through the water.

Swim toward the sunken ships ahead.

Swim down toward the steps and gather the yellow Lums.

Swim inside the sunken ship and keep getting the Lums.

Go on into the corridor ahead.

Surface and go to the ladder in the corner.

Grab the green Lum to save your place.

Look out to spot the other yellow Lums ahead.

Glide to the ledge to the left side of the screen.

Follow the ledge around.

Walk up onto the deck.

Climb up into the ship's rigging.

Jump up on top of the beam.

Whale Bay

Look back toward the mast to spot the red Lums and the purple Lum nearby.

Walk over to the purple Lum and shoot your fist at it. Swing through the red Lums to get the health from them.

Once you have the red Lums, swing back to the beam.

TIP

Make it easy on yourself. When you swing toward the mast, let go and glide down using your chopper ability.

Cross over the mast and walk to the other end of the beam.

Leap and glide over to the ledge.

You can't get any traction on the wet section of the ledge, so slide through the water and grab the yellow Lums.

Leap up to get the higher yellow Lums and to get across the chasms ahead.

Grab the three yellow Lums in front of you when the sliding stops.

TIP

Didn't get all the yellow Lums here the first time? Crawl back up the ship's rigging and go again!

A cave lies to the right of the palm tree ahead.

Enter the cave and you find the warp gate out of this level. However, it still needs to be activated.

Climb back up into the ship's rigging. Shoot your magic fist at the purple Lum and swing out to find another pirate cage in the crow's nest.

Break the cage open and take the five yellow Lums inside.

Glide down into the water and swim around until you find the net hanging on the wall. Climb up the net to discover the cave with the yellow Lums in it to the left.

Glide into the cave but look out for the robo-pirate that jumps on you.

Dodge past the guard to find the final cage on this level.

TIP

With a little effort, you can taunt the robo-pirate and cause him to fall over the ledge into the water below. Once he's there, he'll disappear.

Break the cage open with your magic fist. Follow the Teensie out of the cave. He's headed for the warp gate above.

Go outside the cave and climb up the net to the warp gate cave on the left.

Enter the cave and let the Teensie send you to the Hall of Doors.

Whale Bay

The Sanctuary of Lava and Fire

Enter the new door in the Hall of Doors. The Council of Teensies meets you again and sends you through the next door.

Follow the crack in the earth ahead.

Glide out to grab the red Lum in the air.

Land on the bridge below.

Read the pirate sign to find out this is the Labyrinth.

Follow the ledge to the left.

Walk to the end of the ledge and glide to the other ledge on the left.

Interesting machinery ahead, huh? Get closer to take a better look.

Use your magic fist to blast the robo-pirate that attacks you from the machinery.

Grab the red Lum the robo-pirate leaves behind. Move closer to spot the yellow Lum on the right and the gate set into the stone floor.

The gate set into the stone floor also holds a pirate cage that you can't get to yet.

Bounce on the gate to get up to the next ledge.

Walk up the catwalk.

At the end of the catwalk, you'll find a wooden plank bandage over the tower.

Hit the plank bandage with your magic fist and free the purple Lum inside.

Throw your magic fist out onto the purple Lum and start swinging.

Glide over to the column to grab the first yellow Lum.

Turn around and spot the second wooden plank bandage on the tower.

Throw your magic fist at the second wooden plank bandage to free another purple Lum.

Shoot your magic fist to the first purple Lum. Swing back over to the catwalk by the tower.

The Sanctuary of Lava and Fire

Walk around the catwalk and shoot your magic fist at the second purple Lum. Grab hold and swing around to the side where the yellow Lum is.

Glide over and get the yellow Lum, then take the magic fist power-up. Go back to the catwalk and return to the first purple Lum.

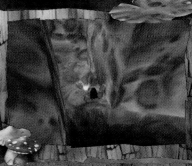

Shoot your magic fist out for the first purple Lum and swing over to the left. Glide down to the ledge where the red Lum waits.

As you get closer to the red Lum, spot the green Lum just a little farther ahead through a crack in the wall.

Glide over to the green Lum and take it.

Keep going forward and around the corner.

Get closer, then prepare to battle the robo-pirate that jumps up at you. Stay on this side of the chasm and wait for the robo-pirate to come to you, firing the whole time.

After the robo-pirate is down, leap and glide across the chasm to the green tree.

Take the red Lum nearby. Keep the wall to the right and walk forward until you spot the cave around the corner.

Glide to the ledge at the cave's entrance.

Leap and glide along the other ledges to follow the passageway.

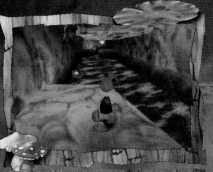

Once you reach the ledge where the green Lum is, shoot the plum from the bush on the wall ahead.

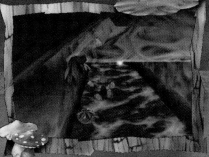

Glide out to the plum and stand on it as it floats on the lava.

You can guide the plum through the lava by throwing your magic fist in the direction opposite from the way you want to go.

Propel the plum to the ledge where the yellow Lum is. Jump up and get it. This entrance is directly across from the tree where you blasted the last robo-pirate. If you look out across the ledge, you'll be able to see the tree and the entrance that took you into the area with the plum trees.

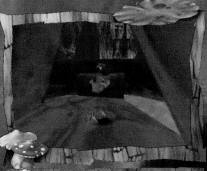

Follow the corridor behind the ledge to reach a large cave.

Jump to the column in the center of the lava pool to get the red Lum. Turn right to spot the plum hanging on the wall. Grab the plum.

NOTE

You can't hit the robo-pirate with the plum close up and get it to stick on its head. It has to be done from a distance.

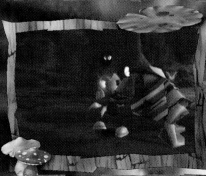

The robo-pirate here is of the indestructible sort. From far away, throw the plum at the robo-pirate.

Once the plum has landed on the robo-pirate's head, run over and leap on it to get up to the ledge where the pirate cage is.

Break the pirate cage open with your magic fist. Take the yellow Lums inside.

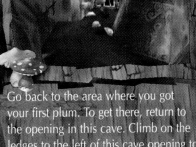

Go back to the area where you got your first plum. To get there, return to the opening in this cave. Climb on the ledges to the left of this cave opening to get the height you need to glide back to the other cave to the left of the tree.

Get another plum and come back through this lava channel again.

The Sanctuary of Lava and Fire

RAYMAN 2
THE GREAT ESCAPE

Keep throwing your magic fist until you get around the lava channel by the tree where you encountered the pirate.

Go through the cave.

In a short time, you're back by the tower where the purple Lums are.

Grab the yellow Lum at the base of the tower near the gate that keeps the cage you spotted earlier.

At the end of the line of red Lums, you'll find another cave you need to enter.

When you reach safe land, hop off the plum.

Take the green Lum beneath the tree, then knock the nearby plum down and pick it up.

Stand back a long distance from the ledge leading out to a lava pool where a spike sticks up. Throw the plum until it lands on the spike.

NOTE

You can't throw the plum on the spike from the ledge's edge. Being close just won't work.

Leap and glide out onto the plum on the spike.

Jump up and grab the ledge and pull up.

Spot the plum in the corner.

Get the plum and throw it toward the spike on the platform.

Leap over after the plum and catch it before it drops off.

TIP

You can't glide between these platforms and get there before the plum drops. So go ahead and start making your way across as soon as you throw the plum. It isn't as hard to get back, and you increase your chances of getting under the plum before it falls. Also, to catch the plum, stand on the shadow under it.

Catch the plum when it comes down.

Turn right and throw the plum toward the next spike.

Hurry and leap across to the next spike—the plum will stay stuck where you are only a short time.

Catch the plum and throw it straight up beside the ledge to the cave. Let the plum drop to the ground between you and the rock face. Jump on the plum and leap up to the ledge.

Pull yourself into the cave above and follow the corridor.

Another pirate cage is just ahead. Break it and take the yellow Lums inside.

If you look up, you'll discover this is the pirate cage under the bouncy gate. Skip the first plum and grab the second one on your way back. Throw it into the air, then throw your magic fist to push you and it into the lava. Go with the lava flow. Return to the cave where you found your very first plum.

Knock another plum down onto the lava. Bounce on the plum on the lava and grab the cobweb against the ceiling and jump to a nearby ledge.

The Sanctuary of Lava and Fire

Leap and glide to the next ledge, then grab the webbing above. Hang there and wait until the baby caterpillars show up.

Blast the baby caterpillars off the webbing and continue forward.

Drop down on the next ledge. Blast the baby caterpiller with your magic fist.

Hit the plum on the wall ahead with your magic fist to knock it into the lava.

Jump on the plum. Shoot the baby caterpillars that attack you.

Leap onto the ledge where the red Lum is.

Keep leaping up the ledges.

Follow the passageway ahead.

Walk forward a little and Murfy shows up with more advice.

Walk to the right to find a plum hanging on a tree. Knock it off the branch with the magic fist.

Jump onto the plum and throw the magic fist toward the tree to propel the plum into the lava.

Instead of going with the flow here, use your magic fist to push yourself backward, past the pirate sign. There's a surprise at the other end of the lava channel.

Keep weaving through the channel until you reach the other end.

Jump off the plum onto the ledge to the right.

Notice the door almost hidden high up on the side of the hill.

Enter the door ahead.

The room in front of you is filled with things you have to do.

Leap across the floating platforms in the lava ahead of you.

Turn right and spot the flamethrower on the ledge. Time the flames, then jump across and head to the left.

Avoid the next flamethrower as well and turn left.

Stand in the middle of the bridge to get a good look at the doors on the back wall.

Jump up in the middle of the bridge and throw your magic fist at the cage on the ledge to the right.

Run across the bridge to the right and leap up onto the ledge where the yellow Lum is waiting. Pull up and look out over the room.

The Sanctuary of Lava and Fire

Drop down to the doorway below. Throw your magic fist against the doors until they break and fly apart.

Enter the room and glide across to the platform in the center of the room.

Look up to spot the stone stalactite formation hanging from the ceiling.

TIP

If you hesitate too long, the stone formation will sink into the lava. Wait around and another will appear to take this one's place. There's no time pressure here except when you go to get across.

Throw your magic fist at the stone formation to knock it loose.

Leap across the fallen stone formation to get to the ledge on the other side.

Follow the corridor around to the left. Turn the corner to the right to spot the next pirate cage.

Turn right and time the flamethrower there. Knock the stone stalactite formation down.

Hop across the stone formation, then glide to the ledge to the left.

Throw your magic fist at the pirate cage to break it. Walk over and grab the yellow Lums.

Leap and glide to the green Lum waiting ahead.

Turn right and walk across the ledges to the column. Glide over to the last platform in front of the columns.

Spot the wooden plank bandages on the two columns ahead and throw your magic fist at them.

Walk across the fallen columns that make bridges through the lava.

Glide through the doorway ahead and land on one of the platforms in the lava.

Grab the green Lum from the first platform, then continue leaping across them. Leap over the flamethrower ahead.

Take the next left, toward the stone stalactite formation hanging from the ceiling.

Throw your magic fist at the stone formation to knock it down. Leap across it to get to the next platform.

The second platform scoots across the lava. Stay on it.

Float toward the cavern below.

When the platform comes to a stop, avoid the flamethrower that tracks you throughout this room. Stay moving to stay ahead of it.

Glide down to the set of pillars on the left.

Jump to the next set of ledges on the right.

Turn right and glide to the next set of ledges.

The Sanctuary of Lava and Fire

Glide to the next set of ledges and climb up. Leap up and blast the pirate cage there with your magic fist. Grab the yellow Lums inside.

Turn left and glide to the ledges there.

Glide to the next ledge and watch out for the small spider waiting for you.

Turn right and walk up the ramp.

After you blast the two spiders here, enter the doorway.

Turn right and walk up the next ramp. Take the red Lum there and spot the purple Lum ahead.

Enter the door here and walk down. Drop onto the ledge below.

Throw your magic fist and grab the purple Lum. Swing up onto the ledge behind the purple Lum and grab the green Lum there.

Turn left and follow the ledge.

Turn right and spot the platforms in the lava below. Glide down to the first platform.

Throw your magic fist at the stone formation hanging from the ceiling, and knock it into the lava. Leap over to it to avoid the flamethrower. Then jump back onto the moving platform again after it's cleared the flamethrower.

Do the same with the next stone formation hanging from the ceiling on the right.

At the end of the ride, leap onto the steps and grab the green Lum there to save your place.

Walk up the steps and turn right. Follow the corridor you find at the top of the steps.

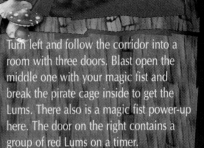

Turn left and follow the corridor into a room with three doors. Blast open the middle one with your magic fist and break the pirate cage inside to get the Lums. There also is a magic fist power-up here. The door on the right contains a group of red Lums on a timer.

Walk to the door on the left and use your magic fist to break through. Blast the giant spider inside.

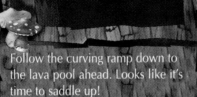

Enter the room and follow the cave down.

Below is a green Lum and a walking shell.

TIP

Walk softly when you reach the floor and the walking shell won't wake up.

Follow the curving ramp down to the lava pool ahead. Looks like it's time to saddle up!

Hiyo, walking shell. Blaze around the ramp!

NOTE

This run through the temple is going to take a lot of work and patience, plus a steady hand. You've got jumps to make, and in one place you have to accelerate the walking shell to get across. It's going to take some serious repetition to get through, but you'll make it.

Memorize the route as you work it. Once you hit the loop-the-loop, you'll actually gain more life than you lose. So after you start consistently getting that far, you don't have to worry about going back to an earlier level when you die.

Try to stay along the inside of the curves rather than the outside. If you bump up against a wall, it generally throws you off for the next turn. A turn or two after you rattle against the walls, the walking shell explodes, taking you with it.

Once you reach the horseshoe-shaped stones ahead, leap off the walking shell and take a breather. You'll have earned it!

Shoot across the burning lava.

The Sanctuary of Lava and Fire

Race around the next ramp.

Leap the gap ahead by jumping on the walking shell, then keep going.

Do a loop-the-loop on the walking shell, then *jump* the next two gaps that come your way. Race into the next cave and across the narrow bridge. Accelerate across the next patch of lava and let off as soon as you're across.

Leap off the walking shell to land on the horseshoe-shaped ridge by the door.

Throw your magic fist at the door to break it apart. Go through.

In the next area, walk to the left and cross the fallen tree.

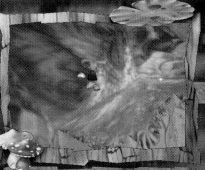

At the end of the fallen tree, glide to the ledge ahead that has the yellow Lums. Grab the yellow Lums.

Glide down into the temple area. Knock the plum from the tree and use it to float back out into the lava. Jump on it on the ground, then use your magic fist to push yourself out onto the lava.

Keep shoving yourself along the lava, past the pirate sign and the tree where you got the plum that brought you into this area.

Go with the lava flow to get the red Lum ahead. Once you turn the corner, you spot even more interesting sights ahead.

Fight the robo-pirate on the bridge ahead.

TIP

When you have to fight while standing on the plum, your best technique is to use the big magic fist. That way you don't get moved around on the plum so much or have to adjust all the time.

Guide your bounce over to the metal ledge on the right.

Leap up from the plum to the metal ledge and pull yourself up.

Follow the tunnel down.

Drop onto the catwalk at the end of the ledge.

Turn left and blast the robo-pirate on the catwalk there.

NOTE
This is the same robo-pirate that confronted you outside. If you didn't blast him then, you'll get the chance now.

Leap and glide across to the catwalk to the left.

Follow the catwalk up to the pirate cage. Break it open with your magic fist and take the yellow Lums inside.

Go back down the catwalk. Glide over to the first catwalk you dropped on, then glide over to the short catwalk in the corner.

Turn left and glide down to the doorway with the green Lum in it.

Enter the next cavern at the back of the ledge.

A spider is also in this room. It's very hard to track down and hit with your magic fist, but get it done otherwise it will cause all kinds of havoc.

The Sanctuary of Lava and Fire

Keep luring the spider out and hit it every chance you get.

Once you finish the spider off, you get a big plum.

Jump on the plum and hop around the room to collect the other red Lums you couldn't get to earlier.

Carry the plum over to the high doorway and throw the plum high into the air.

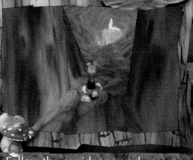

Hop on the plum and leap up through the high doorway.

Follow the corridor around.

Walk through the valley ahead.

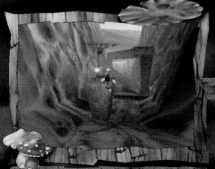

Leap up and glide to the column on the left to get the yellow Lums there.

Walk across the collapsed ruins in front of you and fall through the floor.

Down in the cavern below, you find that you've picked up a plum along the way.

NOTE

If you lose the plum in this area, stay on the ledge. Another plum will be along in just a moment.

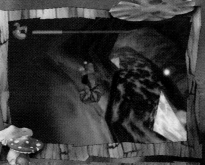

Toss the plum up into the air, then jump on it.

Shoot the magic fist against the back wall to push yourself out toward the lava flow.

Avoid the patches of yellow lava. They burn the plum away and kill you.

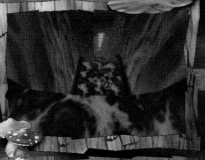

Use the magic fist to shoot yourself and the plum up onto the sloped walls to get the red Lums.

Reverse sides and push yourself to the other side to miss the next yellow lava pit.

Get up high on the next wall and stay there by throwing the magic fist.

Farther down the corridor is a line of red Lums with a yellow Lum and a five-pack of yellow Lums between the doors. Glide to get the red and yellow Lums and land on the plum at the bottom.

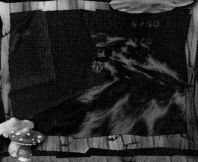

Watch out for the thorned root tentacles that stick out of the wall.

Keep dodging tentacles until you drop through a pit ahead.

Jump off onto the ledge to the left. Take the Lums by knocking the plum from the nearby tree.

TIP

If you don't need the red Lums now, don't get any of them. As you as you get one, the timer starts. You can't get them all now, even from the plum, and the ones you don't get will disappear. Later on you'll come falling out of the small door above you. If the Lums are still here, you'll collect them all as you drop to the ground.

RAYMAN 2
THE GREAT ESCAPE

Be sure to get the line of red Lums to the left of the tree by bouncing on the plum. There is also one green Lum here that you definitely need to get.

NOTE
Don't worry about losing the plum here. If you do, the tree will grow another one.

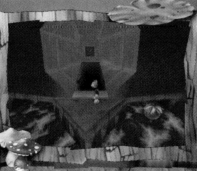

Get back on the plum, then shoot yourself back into the lava flow. Walk to the end of the ledge to avoid the yellow lava beside this ledge.

Use the magic fist to work your way around the yellow lava.

When the lava fall forks, head to the left to get the yellow Lum there.

Leap off the plum and glide to the ledge at the end of the lava flow. Go through the door.

Before you enter the door, listen. You can hear the cry of Lums somewhere nearby. Turn to face the lava flow. Look up, *way* up. Hanging from the cavern ceiling is the last pirate cage. You'll have to travel through a cave you've already passed on this lava flow to reach it. Don't worry, you'll be by this way again.

Blast the caterpillar on the next ledge. Leap out and glide to the magic sphere.

Throw the magic sphere to the ledge with the fire-blasting pyramid. Jump after it.

Throw the magic sphere to the next ledge and follow it again.

Watch out for the baby caterpillars that come out of the darkness. Keep going down in the same fashion.

The next pyramid is a little harder to avoid because it shoots out two cones of fire.

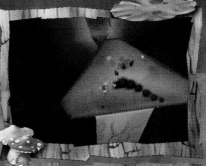

After you throw the magic sphere again and start gliding down, throw the magic fist while you're gliding to blast the caterpillars that creep out to get you.

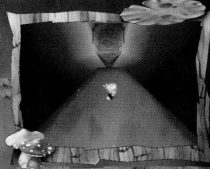

Throw the magic sphere to the doorway ledge ahead.

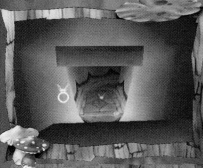

Use the first-person view to spot the purple Lum near the doorway. You won't be able to see it otherwise.

However, ignore this purple Lum and simply glide over to the ledge.

Grab the magic sphere and the green Lum. Follow the corridor ahead.

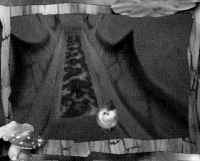

Throw the magic sphere into the air. Shoot the plum in the distance with your magic fist to make it come back to you.

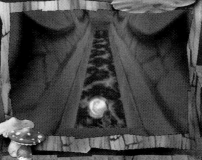

Pick the magic sphere up and step onto the plum.

Throw the magic sphere into the air and shoot your magic fist in the opposite direction to get the plum moving. The magic sphere follows you automatically.

Throw the magic sphere at the ledge ahead, then leap off and glide forward.

The Sanctuary of Lava and Fire

Cross the beam ahead.

Turn left to find the pedestal the magic sphere goes on.

Throw the magic sphere onto the pedestal.

You're given a view of the place where the second magic sphere is.

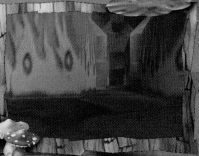

To get the second magic sphere, you're going on another incredible journey. Leap over the lava channel and run to the door on the other side of the room.

Climb up on the ledges and go through the door at the top.

The door at the end of the lava turns to another position, allowing access to another area.

NOTE

Recognize any of this lava? You should, you were here just a little while ago. This is the same lava flow you bobbed along to reach the door that led you to the first magic sphere.

Throw your magic fist at the plum to drop it from the tree to the left.

Put the plum at the edge of the ledge, hop onto it, then blast yourself off into the lava.

As you round the corner notice the yellow lava to your right. The cave entrance is in the wall behind it.

The door out of here is just ahead, but you don't want to go there just yet. See how the lava flows between the wall and the yellow lava on the right? Fire a few magic fists to propel yourself along the wall.

Ease into the cave.

Keep moving until you reach the web-covered rocks. Leave the plum behind as you leap for the webs.

Cobweb just happens to be very springy stuff. Use it to jump from one web to another.

NOTE

The camera angle cannot be changed while you're bouncing up the web stairs. It may feel odd to pull the joystick down to go forward. Take your time making each jump.

When you reach the third web stair look to the right. The wall is covered in webs. Make your next leap toward the wall. Glide to it and hold on, then climb up the web until it ends.

The web ends here on the left side of the cavern wall, but begins again on the wall across from you. Leap up and glide to the next web.

TIP

If you do happen to fall, quickly turn on the ol' chopper. Aim for one of the web stairs and try again.

This is no time to just hang around! Drop to the stone path and follow it.

The familiar plea for help and annoying metal squeal let you know you've found another pirate cage complete with imprisoned Lums. Without dropping off the ledge, fire your magic fist to release the Lums.

The Sanctuary of Lava and Fire

From the edge, look down and to the right in first person view to see the small ledge you must reach. Take a long walk off this short ledge, then kick in the chopper action to glide safely to the ledge below.

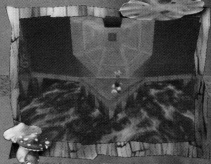

Jump up to the door above and go through.

Once you're through the door, leap onto the plum in front of you.

Start down the lava.

Throw your magic fist straight ahead to knock the doors out of the way at the bottom of the lava.

NOTE

This sequence usually takes a separate attempt to blow the doors open, then glide through.

Glide to the doorway.

Glide onto the columns ahead.

Leap to the green Lum on the ledge once you're past the columns. Follow the corridor down and around.

TIP

Remember, you can pull back on the joystick to slow your sliding rate. Also, grind up against the wall to slow yourself down and use your jumps to position yourself better and slow down as well. Maintain control!

Slide down the ramp and grab the red Lums along the way.

Jump over the flamethrower.

Grab the one yellow Lum along this way. At the end of the ledge, shoot your fist out to grab the purple Lum.

Release the purple Lum and leap to the next ledge. You're greeted by another slide.

Slide down into the next drop.

When you arrive in the next room, you'll spot the next magic sphere to the left. Glide over to it.

Leap up to the block with the magic sphere and take it.

Throw the magic sphere to the floor. Jump and glide around the room and collect the yellow Lum and the red Lums on the ledges. Glide to the middle to get the yellow Lum floating out there.

Go get the magic sphere and put it on its pedestal.

Umber, the guardian of this sanctuary, comes to life and walks out into the middle of the lava channel.

Umber stays in the lava channel.

Shoot your magic fist to the purple Lum and leap up onto the ledge in front of you.

TIP
This is definitely one of the tougher leaps using a purple Lum. You have to get the timing just right. Don't get discouraged and don't fall into the lava.

Glide over to land on Umber's head.

The Sanctuary of Lava and Fire

Umber walks deeper into the lava channel with you on his head.

As Umber approaches the ledge at the end of the lava channel, jump off and glide over to the steps.

Go up the steps.

Follow the ledge around to the left to get the yellow Lum there before you take the next set of steps.

Go up the second set of steps.

Lightning jumps out of you and reaches for the pillar ahead.

The pillar shifts to reveal the second mask inside.

In seconds, you're back with Polokus.

Polokus takes the second mask and places it on his column.

Then Polokus works his magic and sends you back to the Hall of Doors. But the second mask is in place.

The Echoing Caves

Back in the Hall of Doors, enter the Echoing Caves. Watch as a robo-pirate walks through the forested caves.

From your hiding place, watch the robo-pirate walk down into the hole in the ground.

You have a nearby hiding place.

Investigate the buildings first and destroy the robo-pirate on guard there.

Walk up the steps.

Throw your magic fist to flip the switch at the top of the steps.

The tunnel leading down to the pirate cave is still locked. Notice, however, that one of the four lights in the lower right of your screen has come on.

Walk back up the steps and to the ledge overlooking the grounds. Glide over to the hole in the ground that the hint markers keep pointing to.

Don't go in the hole in the ground yet even though the hint markers make it look enticing.

Turn right and spot the five-pack of Lums on the ledge near where you entered. You can't get it yet, but you do need to remember that it's there.

Dive into the hole in the ground. Use your chopper ability to drop down slowly.

Another hint marker points to the water. Wait on that for a moment.

Turn left and knock the plum loose.

Take the plum to the door to the right of the pool.

Stand on the foot of the steps and throw the plum onto the robo-pirate's head at the back of the room.

Run up to the robo-pirate and jump onto his head and scale the nets behind him.

Leap from one net on the wall to the other and keep going up.

Climb up the ledge and grab the five-pack of yellow Lums here.

Dive into the pool.

Swim through the cave underwater.

Turn left and swim through the doorway.

Leap out onto the next ledge.

In the next room, look up to spot the next ledge on the wall to the left of the window. Use your magic fist to activate the switch.

Return through the pool and climb back up on the robo-pirate and the nets. Leap out into the open area. Run past the locked pirate door in the ground.

Leap out on the column before you.

Glide to the next column to the right.

Leap to the ledge.

Walk to the left and investigate the magic stone there.

TIP

The door is closed by four switches.

Look behind the big tree ahead to find another five-pack of yellow Lums. *These Lums are easily missed!*

The hint markers swirl into another arrow at the ledge in front of you.

Glide to the green Lum at the bottom of the buildings in front of you.

Turn left and spot the switch there. Use your magic fist to activate it. This isn't one of the four you need to find, but it does raise the platforms in the water so you can get back up.

The Echoing Caves

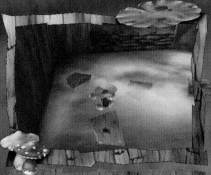

Cross to the other end of the boardwalk and leap across the boards floating in the pond. You can also wade—there's nothing to worry about in the water—but that's just not as cool!

Blast the robo-pirate waiting for you on the other side of the pond.

Jump up and throw your magic fist at the switch on the wall that the robo-pirate was guarding.

TIP
Stand at the far end of the board-walk here, leap up, and hit the switch with your magic fist to acti-vate the platforms. It will add a few seconds to your time.

Cross back over to the button that raises the platforms out in the pond. It's on a timer, so you have to hurry across them.

While crossing the platforms, leap without gliding to save time.

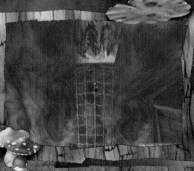

Climb up the net to the opening above.

Follow the corridor around to a clearing with floating platforms lead-ing up to a high building. Grab the green Lum ahead to save your place.

Hop onto each of the platforms and let them rise to get to the proper jumping distance. The first one has yellow Lums at the top. However, once you have the Lums, the platform will turn over. Stay on your toes and glide to the next platform.

Once you're on the other ledge, walk to the left and up the netting there.

Enter the building and follow the corridor around.

Hit the switch in front of you to open the door to the left. It's on a timer, so hurry.

The last switch is right around the corner. Throw your magic fist to activate it.

Walk forward to find the five-pack of yellow Lums ahead.

Jump back down to the pirate door set in the ground.

Enter the open door and walk forward until you fall over the ledge.

Walk forward and grab the powder keg in the center of the room.

Take the powder keg back to the room where you arrived. Throw the powder keg at the plank bandage. Throw your magic fist at the pirate cage hidden there. Take the red Lums inside.

The other end of the room lets out onto an underground pool. Jumping into the water is not a good idea. You're going to need something to help you get across the water.

Grab the nearby powder keg and walk over to the torch.

As soon as the powder in the keg ignites, the barrel takes off like a rocket. Hang onto it and guide it across the water with the D-pad.

NOTE

It may take some repeated trips through this area to get all the Lums ahead. Plus it can be tough to land at the other end. You've saved your progress here, so learn to live through the adventure by doing it.

Land in the mast section ahead by aiming to the right of the mast. Spot the next pirate cage above during your trip.

Pull up on the mast ledge and take the nearby Lums. *Don't* touch the nearby powder keg or you'll be gone before you get the chance to get the pirate cage.

The Echoing Caves

Turn left and quickly leap across the wooden section there because it will drop away beneath you.

Climb up the net to the ledges where the pirate cage is. Break the cage open and get the yellow Lums inside.

Leap over to the pirate trampoline against the wall and glide over to the ledge above.

Walk around behind the mast to get the yellow Lums from the ledges there.

Glide down to the powder keg below. Hold it to the nearby torch and take off.

Grab the yellow Lums along the way. A yellow Lum is on the right of the first pole that you encounter. It can be easy to miss.

Keep streaking forward and gather the yellow Lums along the way. Land on the ledge at the end of the line of yellow Lums.

NOTE

There is a lower ledge here that's easier to get to, but this one is a natural stopping point if you're going to get all the yellow Lums. You really want to get here because you'll find an entrance that leads to the Fairy Glade where you found the one pirate cage you couldn't get to when you were in that level.

Super Secret Entrance to Fairy Glade!

At the end of this corridor is a special exit that leads to the Fairy Glade.

Look through the gnarly bars ahead to spot the building that holds the pirate cage you couldn't get into the first time.

Turn around and drop down the tunnel.

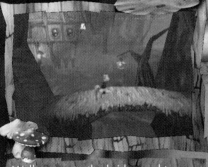

Walk out onto the bridge and turn left to spot the plum. Throw your magic fist to knock the plum loose.

Leap from the bridge and glide over to the plum.

Throw your magic fist to float under the bridge and around the corner.

Leap up for the red Lum and hang onto the cobweb there.

Climb along the cobweb and glide onto the platform below.

Leap along the platforms. Blast the baby caterpillars that attack you.

Jump up and grab hold of the cobweb over your head. Blast the baby caterpillars and climb along the cobweb to the purple Lum ahead.

Drop down to the green Lum ahead.

Jump up and throw your magic fist at the first of three purple Lums ahead. Swing over and throw your magic fist at the next and swing again.

The Echoing Caves

Glide to the platform ahead.

Throw your magic fist at the next purple Lum and keep going.

Make your way around the platforms and purple Lums the same way.

Look out for the robo-pirate standing on the ledge above.

Don't try to fight the robo-pirate yet. Glide over to the ledge.

Stand on the bridge to the right and let the robo-pirate blast the left bridge to pieces. Grab the open door that appears there.

Pull into the doorway and follow the hallway into a room with a sleeping pirate.

There's plenty of room for fighting the robo-pirate here, so get to it! When you're finished, walk to the left and look out the window to spot the last pirate cage on this level. Blast the pirate cage and the two yellow Lums will come to you, allowing you to mark the Fairy Glade as finished.

The hole in front of the robo-pirate's chair will drop you back into the Echoing Caves.

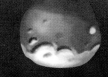

Back in the Echoing Caves

Back in the Echoing Cave, walk to the front of the tunnel and glide down to the right of the screen where the robo-pirate is on guard.

Grab the green Lum and run toward the water so the robo-pirate will follow you. Leap up and let him run under you at the edge. He'll short-circuit.

The door the robo-pirate was guarding is locked and even the nearby powder keg won't let you in.

Walk to the ledge at the front of this entrance. Turn right and leap to that ledge.

Cross the big rock and leap to the next bridge.

Spot the switch on the wall above and ahead. However, you can't quite get to it.

Return to the locked door and get the powder keg. Use the torch to ignite the powder keg and ride it up into the switch.

Once the switch is active, make your way back around the ledges to where the locked door was.

Go through the door.

Throw the powder keg you get in this new level straight up to hit the pirate cage overhead. You'll get a shower of red Lums.

Take another powder keg and stand close to the torch to launch again. Grab the yellow Lums along the way.

Race through the water-filled tunnel ahead and control your flight with the D-pad as usual.

The Echoing Caves

A door opens at the other end.

Race to the ledge across the room and hop off the powder keg.

The robo-pirate in the next room is one maladjusted sailor!

Look at the wall to the right to spot the switch there. You'll be getting back to that later.

Leap onto the ledge and battle the robo-pirate until you put him down.

Turn around until you spot the five-pack of yellow Lums on the net to the right of the door you came through.

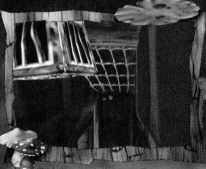

Bounce up and grab the net overhead. Walk along it until you reach the pirate cage hanging from the net. Break it open.

Climb back along the net and drop and glide down to the ledge where you battled the robo-pirate. Head back out to where the timer button operating the gate is. Throw your magic fist from the doorway to save yourself some steps.

TIP

When you're operating the timer switch here, throw from the doorway leading to the bridge where you fought the robo-pirate. It will save you some time.

Jump back to the bridge where you fought the robo-pirate. Run to the other end of the bridge where the powder keg is and pick it up.

Run the powder keg to the torch at the end of the bridge and ignite. Ignore the door on the right and fly through the door you came in.

Fly through this tunnel and collect the yellow Lums along the way. This path is actually different than the way you got here.

Fly up to the net at the end of this ballistic ride.

The net starts to fall as soon as you're on it. Climb left quickly and leap onto the ledge to the left.

NOTE

You're going to see more nets like this one. Learn how to climb them now. To move swiftly, use jumps mixed in with your movements. The jumps let the nets last a little longer and you definitely cover more ground.

Land on the ledge with the green Lum to save your place.

Hurry along the ledges because they'll fall out from under you. Take the powder keg with you to the next ledge. Be sure to get the yellow Lums along the way.

Hang onto the ledge when the powder keg blows and pull yourself up. Walk around the ledge until you can see the pirate cage there. Throw your magic fist at it to break it and release the Teensie inside.

Join the Teensie to open the warp gate to the Hall of Doors. Jump through.

The Echoing Caves

The Precipice

Meanwhile, back at the pirate ship...

Captain Razorbeard isn't a happy camper when he finds out Rayman has gotten two of the masks.

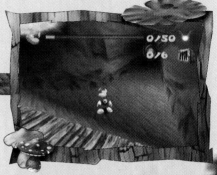

Things get tense on this level immediately. Watch as the pirate ship blows the bridge away in front of you.

Run to the left and get the yellow Lum there.

Follow the ledge around the mountain but keep moving because the ledges fall away behind you. If you stop on them, you're going down too!

Jump up into the net around the next corner.

Crawl along the net and drop to the next ledge. Dodge the walking shell that comes at you.

Continue around the ledge and leap the gaps that the pirate ship blows out. Dodge another walking shell.

NOTE

Even when the pirate ship blows sections of the bridge out, you can still leap from them. Don't give up. Attempt to leap toward your goal or activate your chopper ability and glide toward it.

Throw your magic fist at the purple Lum and swing across to the green Lum. Glide down to the ledge below and keep running.

Run to the net on the wall ahead. As soon as you start crawling on the net, it starts to fall. Get up high enough and glide over to the next ledge. Dodge another walking shell.

Run around the corner quickly or the pirate ship will blow the ledges out from under you. Also, the one at the corner will drop away as you cross over it, so don't hesitate.

The structure built into the wall looks stable, but it starts to fall as soon as you set foot on it. Run across it.

Keep running across the next bridge because it will break away as well. Leap out and glide to the next bridge. Don't miss the green Lum hanging in the air. A pirate cage hangs above you.

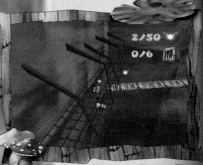

You can't get to the cage here, so continue running around the corner. Leap up into the nets and climb along.

Glide down to the next bridge. Run quickly because the robo-pirates will shoot the bridge out from beneath you.

Run across the bridge and watch out for the walking shell. A purple Lum is ahead.

Throw your magic fist at the purple Lum and swing across to the next bridge and the green Lum waiting there.

Another pirate cage is around the next corner.

Leap up and shoot the cage with your magic fist to break it. Keep running.

The Precipice

Avoid the next walking shell by flipping over it, then leap out to seize the net on the wall. The net starts falling almost immediately. Leap and glide out to the bridge on the right. Don't forget the yellow Lum here.

At the end of the next bridge, leap out onto the net on the wall. Cross it and leap out onto the second net on the right. Cross and leap out onto the bridge ahead.

Throw your magic fist at the red switch ahead to shut down the electrified door. Then break open the pirate cage here.

Go through the door.

More bridges lie ahead, these across water. Get moving!

Beware of walking shells and cannonballs that knock the bridge out from beneath you. When you see a cannonball hit the bridge, get ready to jump because that section is going to disappear.

CAUTION
The trampoline is on a timer. You only get three or four bounces before it disappears.

Follow the bridge up and around the building ahead. Even as you start to go up the bridge, the building starts sinking into the water.

Bounce on the trampoline ahead to get to the next level.

Run around the building in the other direction. Grab onto the overhead net to get across to the next section.

Drop down onto the next section of the bridge and keep going.

Climb around the next net section and get to the sinking bridge section before it goes completely under.

Use the trampoline at the end of the next net section to bounce up to the next level.

Up this section of the bridge, with cannonballs flying all around you, is another trampoline. Use it to get up to the next level.

As you run up this bridge section, jump over the rolling powder kegs and keep going.

Leap on top of the powder keg dispenser and *glide* onto the net behind it.

Jump from the net out onto the next trampoline. Bounce up to the next level.

Pull yourself up to the ledge where the yellow Lums are and keep going.

Run around the corner to get a magic fist power-up and another pirate cage. A second pirate cage is behind the first one. Break them both.

NOTE

This is one of those really tough spots where you kind of have to depend on the repeat function of the game. It's hard to get both pirate cages here without dying at least a few times.

Jump up and go around the two nets here.

The Precipice

Leap out onto the ledges ahead and climb up.

Use your magic fist to blast the robo-pirate and the switch behind him.

Climb the rope ladder the electrified gate was guarding to find another pirate cage. Break it open.

Blast the switch here to move the boom arm into position so you can go along it.

Gather the yellow Lums along the boom arm.

Run back to the other end of the boom arm to enter the doorway on the ship there.

Glide down to the bridge below and start running.

Follow the ledge along, dodging the usual assortment of deadly things, and jump up to grab the net overhead.

TIP

In this area, on the sections that are struck by cannonballs and drop away, simply try staying close to the side of the mountain and running straight ahead. You'll be blown up into the air, but most of the time you'll stay moving and on track!

Keep running along the bridge and cross the two other net areas as well. At the end of the third net, leap into the hole in the side of the mountain.

TIP

Stay in the center of the nets as you crawl to the right. If you go up too high, you'll jump off and end up in the water.

Drop down into the pit and spot all the Lums ahead.

Glide to get all the yellow Lums.

Dodge or use your magic fist to knock out the flying explosives that attack you. Continue grabbing Lums.

Keep grabbing Lums and land on the ledge below.

Run along the ledge and leap out to get to the next one while the pirate ship fires at you.

Notice that the second bridge isn't against the stone wall. If you're not careful you'll miss it. Run along and leap the blown sections of the bridge while avoiding a steady supply of walking shells.

Run forward and glide into the door in the mountainside ahead.

Enter the door and go forward.

Go through the door ahead.

Now this looks like a dangerous place!

Walk toward the red Lum and cross the huge dock. Blast the robo-pirate that confronts you. He's the biggest and baddest you've ever faced.

Stay down in the big area and keep moving. If you let this robo-pirate close enough to use his hook, he'll kill you in one evil swipe. Stay away and dance, firing every chance you get. After you defeat him, the door he's guarding opens.

The Precipice

Don't enter this door immediately. Run to the left of it instead, around the corner to find the ledge there.

Run up the ramp to enter a passageway.

Inside the passageway, two five-packs of Lums hang over your head. Stand underneath them and they will come down to you.

Enter the newly opened doors to save the Teensie in the last cage on this level. Walk into the room with him.

The Teensie opens the warp gate to get you back to the Hall of Doors.

The Top of the World

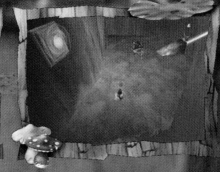

The robo-pirates on this level have real problems.

However, they certainly look fierce enough to take you easily!

Hop on the chair behind the robo-pirate to take off for the ride of your life!

Zip through the trees ahead and gather the yellow Lums along the way. Use the D-pad to go round and round to collect the Lums and to avoid obstacles.

Round and round and round you go.

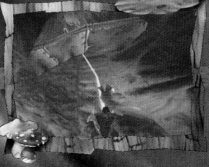

Just avoid those sudden, painful stops!

This is one of the most exciting trips yet.

Locked doors open in front of you as you approach.

Beware of the armed robot sensors waiting to ambush you ahead. You can throw your magic fist at them. Keep gathering the Lums along the way.

At the end of the ride, an alarm sounds. Watch out for the barrel-shaped guard lumbering your way.

To put this guy away quickly, stand by the wall and shoot your magic fist at the back wall and ricochet it into your enemy. That way you won't even be touched by his attack.

Walk down the hallway where the barrel-shaped guard came from. Take the yellow Lum on the right.

TIP

If you're short on life, you can walk really close behind the barrel-shaped guard and he won't see you. You can duck into the closet area with the yellow Lum and wait for him to walk back the other way, then slip past him and keep going.

Ahead, you can see barrels rolling past the door. Go through the door.

The barrels smash against the wall to the right, so go left. Hop over the barrels and look for the door-way on the right.

Enter the doorway.

Climb the net on the right side of the wall.

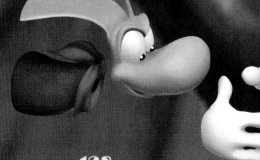

Climb the ledge at the top. Follow the corridor around to the green Lum at the entrance to a new room. Turn to the right and pick up the powder keg.

Carry the powder keg to the barrel-shaped guard in the room and heave it at him. In seconds, he's just hoops and splinters.

Go get the red Lums left behind by the barrel-shaped guard. Turn right to spot the first pirate cage on this level.

Break the pirate cage open and take the yellow Lums inside.

Keep the crates to your right and walk forward. Spot the yellow Lum in the doorway on the right, but don't get it yet.

Keep going forward and pull up onto the crate in front of you.

Turn left and cross the crate to get the yellow Lum on top. Farther ahead and on the right is another yellow Lum. Be careful getting it because it hangs over a pit that leads to certain death.

Leap and glide over the pit to get the yellow Lum.

Turn around and leap back over the pit.

Walk forward until you spot the door on the left.

The room at the end of this short corridor has a platform that flips over. Enter the room.

The platform floats under a yellow Lum. Unfortunately, the platform then turns over and becomes deadly. But there is a ledge on the left on the back wall.

The Top of the World

The floating platform is a deathtrap. Simply jump up and catch the cobweb on the ceiling above.

NOTE

If you're stuck in this area because you've been trying to make the platform work for you, now you know why. If you've been up to the warp gate later in this level, here's the secret to that too! Man, the things you miss when you choose the obvious route!

Turn right and spot the path. Climb over there.

Follow the hallway.

The door at the end of this corridor has a wooden plank bandage over it. Your magic fist won't work against it.

Go back and get a powder keg. Bring it back to the platform and walk on.

At the other end of the ride, walk off down the path you found with the cobweb.

Throw the powder keg at the door. Go through the door.

Another yellow Lum, a magic fist power-up, and a Teensie are in this room. Jump down and get them. The Teensie immediately disappears. But he's going where you're going to need him later.

Climb back up the crates where the Teensie went out. Follow him.

Use the cobweb to get back to the big room. Keep going until you get back to the room with the yellow Lum that you passed up earlier.

Grab the yellow Lum and climb the net on the wall.

Follow the corridor at the top of your climb. Another barrel-shaped guard beats a path through the hallway.

TIP

If you just can't make the hallway without dying at the hands of the barrel-shaped guard, there is a way to eliminate the threat. With a little care, you can inch your way around the corner until there is just enough room to throw your magic fist into the hallway with the barrel-shaped guard. Blast him into kindling.

When the barrel-shaped guard walks to the left, cut around the corner to the right and get the two yellow Lums there. Go hide back in the hallway.

This time when the barrel-shaped guard walks to the right, cut around the corner to the left. A red carpet is spread across the floor in this room.

Follow the red carpet to the steps.

Go up the steps to spot the locked door at the top. No doubt your barrel-shaped friend is the key to getting this opened.

Go back into the room and attack the barrel-shaped guard with your blistering ricochet attack.

Once the guard is down, get the red Lums left behind. Another yellow Lum is at the end of the short corridor at the foot of the red carpet.

The second cage on this level is ahead and on the right. Break it open with your magic fist and get the yellow Lums inside.

Climb up the short crate in this area.

Turn around until you spot the yellow Lum on top of the crates.

Leap across to get the yellow Lum on the crates.

The Top of the World

Turn around and spot the yellow Lum in the opposite corner on the crates. Go get it. Use the short crate at the end of the line on the left there.

Walk up to the closed doors and they'll open. Follow the corridor to get to the warp gate and break out your dancing shoes.

When the Teensie activates the warp gate for you, jump in to get to the Hall of Doors. Enter the Sanctuary of Rock and Stone.

The Walk of Power

When you arrive from the warp gate, turn left to find the fairy Ly waiting for another race. Enter the ring of rocks and get ready.

Race alongside Ly to get the yellow Lums in the cavern.

Keep following Ly across the streams.

Glide to the right to reach the first time extension.

Keep running and grabbing the yellow Lums. Head up the incline after Ly.

Leap onto the lily pads going by in the stream ahead. Don't go into the water.

Jump off the lily pad to the right and follow Ly.

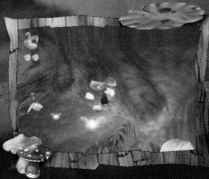

Jump across the three chasms ahead and keep going.

Leap across the lily pads out in the big pond. Keep Ly in your sights.

NOTE

Remember, you can go through this level several times if necessary to get all the Lums. It's important that you beat the timed race. Once you start learning the course, stay ahead of Ly if you can and let her catch up when you reach areas you don't know. During the course that you know, you'll find short cuts. Remember, use the glide maneuver sparingly to save time.

Head immediately for the lily pad with the time extension on it.

Turn and jump from lily pad to lily pad to keep following Ly.

TIP

Lead the lily pads a little while they approach. It's better to be on them early and waiting than watching them leave as you hit the water. You've got to shave seconds everywhere you can now.

The last lily pad lets you out onto a narrow spit of land. There are only two more small jumps between you and the winner's spot. The first comes at the end of this spit of land. And the second is the short ledge right in front of the magic stone where Ly is. Ly decides to reward you with more power. You get a stronger magic fist.

NOTE

Remember, getting all 50 yellow Lums on this level is important. Without them you won't be able to finish the game.

Then a Teensie arrives to take you back to the Hall of Doors.

The Teensie does his dance and you warp out of there. Enter the Sanctuary of Rock and Stone.

The Sanctuary of Rock and Stone

This time walk forward along the bridge.

Leap over to the next section of bridge and keep going.

Leap out onto the net stretched tight before you.

When the big robo-pirate shows up, put those new magic fists of yours to work.

Jump and glide onto the barrel floating beside the net.

Float along but beware of the ghosts that come up from the water. Blast them with your magic fist.

Leap out onto the ledge to the right when the barrel slows down. Jump quickly because it's going to sink. Grab the green Lum there to save your place.

Walk up the ledge and spot the exploding barrels rolling down the bridge ahead. Leap over them and go up the bridge here.

Get the timing down and leap over the barrels as you climb this bridge.

When you reach the hatch that's rolling the barrels out, leap to the left and get on the ledge there.

Leap through the window with the green Lum.

The water below looks really dangerous.

Glide down to the tree lying in the water.

Watch out for the huge creature that's got its eye on you!

Go to the right fork of the tree first to get the red Lum there. Watch out for the leaping piranha.

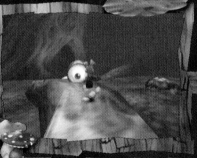

Take the left fork this time. Follow the bouncing eye ball! Hit it with your magic fist to get it out of the way.

Follow the path of the next eyeball.

Keep gliding around on the tree roots.

Turn left and glide onto the turtle shell.

Glide along the turtle shells, then out onto the broken bridge.

Jump down to the next section of bridge. Stay there for a moment.

Turn around and look up to spot the first pirate cage on this level. Break it with your magic fist and free the purple Lum inside.

Swing across the broken section of bridge on the purple Lum.

Gather the green Lum along the way as you head for the temple.

Turn left and look up to spot the magic fist power-up there.

Glide over to the stone by the magic fist power-up. Jump up and take the power-up.

Glide to the main temple stone path. Look out for the robo-pirate who attacks immediately.

Your powered fists make short work of this robo-pirate. But notice the bouncing eyeball next to him.

Inside the room is a festival of bouncing eyeballs. So which way do you go now?

Throw your magic fist to burst all the eyeballs and clear the way. Enter the room. These bloodshot eyeballs are actually camouflage for the yellow Lums behind them. Blast the eyeballs to reveal the hidden prizes and gather them up.

Go through the door in the back.

Follow the corridor.

Spot this level's second pirate cage up by all the caterpillars.

The Sanctuary of Rock and Stone

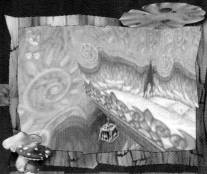

Use your magic fist to blast all the caterpillars. Get the green Lum here as well. You can't get the pirate cage yet.

Go up the ramp in the back right corner.

Climb up onto the bridge where the pirate cage is.

Jump over the side of the bridge and use your chopper ability. Blast the pirate cage with your magic fist on the way down. Grab the five-pack of Lums as you go.

Climb up to the bridge again and go through the door at the other end.

Blast all the caterpillars in the next room to clear them out of the way.

Leap to the ledge to the right.

The yellow Lums positioned at the top of the wall look interesting.

The stained glass window on the other side of the room is intriguing, too. But there's a ledge ahead and to the right along that wall.

Climb the wall where the yellow Lums are and take them.

Drop to the ledge below and follow the corridor ahead.

Watch out for the tentacles sticking out of the wall around the corner.

Hit the tentacle with your magic fist to make it pull back into the wall.

Run forward and around the corner to find another one. Throw your magic fist at it too, then glide over the gap.

Don't go forward yet. Turn around and spot the pirate cage behind you in the nook of the stone wall.

Jump up and break the pirate cage with your magic fist. The freed yellow Lums won't come to you, and you can't jump back across this gap. For now leave them there.

Keep following the passageway.

Around the next corner is a pit with a blue flower in it. Hit the tentacle with your magic fist to make it go away.

Enter the room and take all the Lums against the wall and on both sides of the steps.

Leap onto the blue flower to get it moving. Use your magic fist to stun the tentacles before they can reach you.

Grab the yellow Lums as you go by.

Float back into the room with the stained glass window.

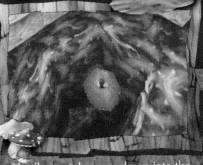

The flower takes you down into the gaping pit in the center of the room.

TIP

If you get knocked off the blue flower along your float trip, there are a number of places where you can simply jump back onto it. But once it's gone down the pit, it's gone.

The Sanctuary of Rock and Stone

RAYMAN 2
THE GREAT ESCAPE

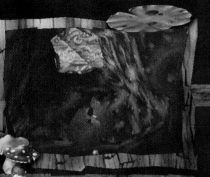

CAUTION

If you don't blast this underground door open with your magic fist before you reach it, you'll die!

After a long descent, you arrive in a cave with an impressive door.

Blast the door open with your magic fist before it can kill you.

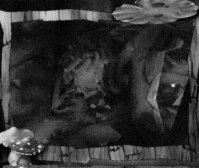

Ahead is another chamber. It holds a green Lum, but watch out for the flamethrower on the right.

The flamethrower torches your pretty blue flower out from under you. Leap to the ledge where the green Lum is to save your progress.

Jump up and glide to the new flower ahead.

Grab the next yellow Lum even as your flower is set on fire.

While this flower burns, leap and glide to the next.

Start blasting the door ahead so you can get through.

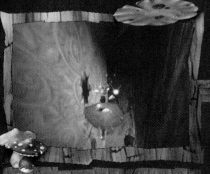

Float into the open chamber behind the broken door. Stun the tentacles that stick through the sides of the wall. Grab the yellow Lums.

When the flower fades beneath you, use your chopper ability to glide down and grab the yellow Lums below. Land on the ledge.

Enter the door behind you and take a look around.

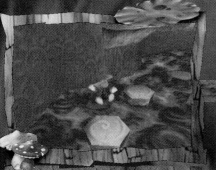

Glide from platform to platform across the lava. Keep moving because they sink after only a short while!

Ahead and to the left against the wall you'll find another pirate cage. You'll have to break it by throwing your magic fist while crossing the platforms in the lava. Throw and glide in one move, then repeat.

Glide over to the green ledge where the yellow Lum is.

Time the flamethrower, then glide over to the other green ledge to get the yellow Lums freed from the pirate cage. Notice the tentacles that suddenly break through the wall behind you. Throw your magic fist to stun the tentacles, then glide over to the ledge and run.

At the other end of the ledge, you can see a door in the wall. To the left of the door is a switch.

Throw your magic fist to hit the switch. A platform extends before the ledge with the door, making the distance something you can make. But it's on a timer so you'll have to hurry.

Run and glide over to the ledge extension and keep moving for the door.

Enter the door.

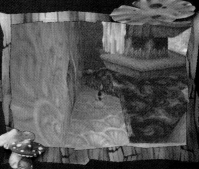

The next area you enter is even more dangerous.

The Sanctuary of Rock and Stone

Forget about the turning platform in the middle of everything for a moment. Turn left and follow the ledge there.

Leap up onto the green ledge where the yellow Lum is.

Glide over to the yellow Lum on the turning platform.

Once you're on the turning platform, run away from the lava flow and wait until it stops briefly.

TIP

It's easiest to stay ahead of the lava flow if you stay close to the inside of the turn. Don't try to run around at the edges.

Glide to the green ledge behind the turning platform.

Climb the wall to get the yellow Lums at the top.

Continue climbing to the left on the wall.

Drop down onto the green ledge and turn around to spot the pirate cage on the wall across the room. Break the cage with your magic fist and wait on the ledge until the Lums come to you.

Turn left to spot the door, the timed switch, and the green Lum on the ledge.

Glide down to the upper arm of the turning platform, then wait until you're under the ledge to jump up and grab it.

TIP

Your timing usually works best if you throw the magic fist just as the turning platform's upper arm swings into view on the right side of your screen.

Pull up onto the smaller platforms above the turning one.

Hit the timer beside the door with your magic fist. Grab the yellow Lum and race through the door before it can close.

Take the green Lum inside the next room. Turn right and follow the corridor. Blast the baby caterpillars that float down and attack you.

On the ledge ahead, a tentacle rips up through the ground. Notice the switch on the wall to the right.

Throw the magic fist at the tentacle and glide across. Now throw the magic fist at the timed switch until the door opens all the way. You hit it once and it only opens a little. You can't get through then.

TIP

You have to hit the timed switch on this ledge several times to get it open all the way. Otherwise you'll never get through the door.

When the door is open all the way, glide across and go through.

On the ledge behind the door, look down and to the left to spot another pirate cage. Walk around the railing in front of you and turn at the corner. Throw the magic fist from here to explode the cage. Wait for the yellow Lums to come up to you.

Turn right and follow the ramp down. As soon as you start down, a massive section of the wall pushes out, blocking your way.

Turn left and spot the two yellow Lums above a column. Leap out and glide down to grab the Lums, then land on the column.

When you land on the column, turn left and leap onto the wall. Climb the wall to safety.

The Sanctuary of Rock and Stone

Back at the wall section, stand around for a moment to discover that it's actually timed. It goes in and out. Wait until it's on its way back into the wall, then leap over and run. Hop on the column in the lava and keep going.

Around the corner are a green Lum and more moving walls.

Time the walls so they're staggered. They don't move at the same speed. When the one on the right is pulling back, the one on the left should just be finishing going forward, ready to go back. Run and leap through them.

In case you get caught in a pinch, you can also hang from the ledge's side briefly.

Leap onto the columns sticking up from the lava. Throw your magic fist at the switch on the wall while you're leaping through them.

Hitting the timer switch moves the massive block on the left.

Run past the massive stone block and through the open door.

At the end of this corridor is the last pirate cage and the warp gate.

Don't walk up the steps yet. Walk over to the columns to the left and the right and look behind them to find the final two yellow Lums to complete your collection on this level.

Throw the magic fist at the warp gate to bounce it up into the pirate cage and break it.

Join the Teensie in the victory dance.

Jump into the warp and go to the Hall of Doors. Go to the entrance to Beneath the Sanctuary of Rock and Stone.

Beneath The Sanctuary of Rock and Stone

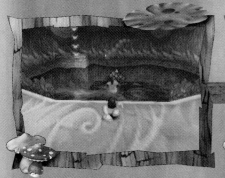

After another brief meeting with the Teensie Council, you find yourself in yet another world.

Walk over to the magic stone to find the words of wisdom there. Throw your magic fist at the caterpillar until it's gone.

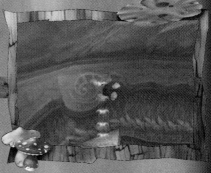

Use your new super chopper to fly out to the ledge where the five red Lums are hovering. Land on the ledge.

Fly off the ledge and across the lava pit. Alternate flying with throwing your magic fist to break the door under the ledge.

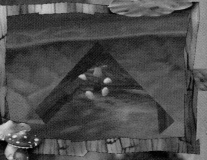

Fly through the door and follow the tunnel ahead.

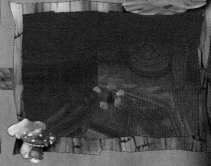

Turn left and fly to the ledge. Stop flying and walk around. Follow the corridor but watch out for the spikes that shoot out.

Find a pirate cage at the end of the ledge. Use your magic fist to break it open. Stay there and let the yellow Lums come to you.

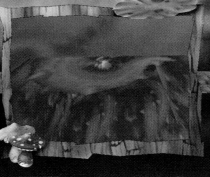

Walk back around the ledge and fly out into the big room you arrived in again. This time fly up into the hole in the ceiling.

Blast the baby caterpillars in the cobwebs inside the hole in the ceiling, but don't drop to the thorny ground. Follow the passageway.

Avoid the green tentacle and keep flying. Land on the green ledge and walk out to get the green Lum to save your place.

Fly out into the airstream generated by the fan and glide through the door beside the flamethrower when the way is clear. There's plenty of room to fly over the flames. Grab the Lum as you go through.

Glide through the passage and through the next tunnel. Keep going into the next cavern with the lava fall. Blast the baby caterpillars that come at you.

Land on the ledge where the green Lum is to save your place.

In the next room, fly under the thorny tentacles and time the flamethrowers so you don't get burned as you pass through. It's really easier than it looks and the major threat is from the thorns.

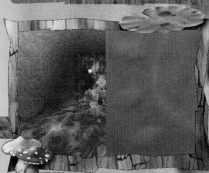

Around the corner to the left after flying through the next opening, watch out for the tentacles that explode from the wall. Grab the green Lum to save your place.

Throw your magic fist at the next door to blow it open. Fly through.

Weave around the lava falls in the next room.

Blast the next door open with your magic fist and go through. Dodge through the lava in the next chamber, then take the yellow Lums from the platforms. If you want to rest for a minute, stop on one of the platforms.

Fly to the ledge to the left. Gather the Lums along the way.

Look under the path where it goes over the lava to spot a pirate cage there.

Go to the doorway to get the green Lum. Turn around and get a better look at the pirate cage behind you.

Use your magic fist to break the pirate cage, then walk back up the path and fly down so the yellow Lums will come to you.

Fly back into the room and get the yellow Lum floating high in the air.

Land on the ground and blast all the baby caterpillars that come at you.

Fly up in front of the green stalactite in front of you. Throw the magic fist so that it bounces onto the door below and breaks it open.

Before you go through the open door, fly behind the green stalactite to get the five-pack of yellow Lums hiding there. Then fly through the door.

On the next ledge, leap up and fly along the airstream created by the fan behind you. Weave through the lava spills ahead and grab the yellow Lums along the way. At the three lava falls, swing to the right to grab the yellow Lum there.

NOTE

If you die and have to start over in front of the fan (and you've already gotten the yellow Lum on the right of the lava fall), there's an easier route through the falls. Float between the first and second lava spill of the first three. Stay to the left and drop altitude to float between the next lava fall and the wall. Float up against the ceiling and weave back and forth between the next lava spills until you reach the end.

Grab the yellow Lum ahead and follow the corridor down.

CAUTION

If you hit the ceiling while you're flying, you'll be bounced off. A lot of times you'll end up in the lava below. Pull the control stick back to slow your progress.

Float along the next passage. Be alert for Lums.

27/50

From the green Lum, you have to drop a lot of altitude, barely skimming above the surface of the lava, to get through the next opening. Get the yellow Lum under the overhang ahead.

773/999   66/80

RESUME GAME

LOAD

OPTIONS

After you get the green Lum and go through the low opening, grab the yellow Lum over the first then the second bridges, and cut hard left over the third bridge structure to find a secret room along this passageway. It's marked by a golden light that stands out against the red lava.

Beneath The Sanctuary of Rock and Stone

RAYMAN 2
THE GREAT ESCAPE

NOTE

This secret entrance can be really tricky to find. After you do the low dive to get under the first bridge after getting the green Lum, the secret room opening will be on the left, three bridges down. You have to start maneuvering early to get on the ledge there, and it may take a number of attempts to get it.

Two pirate cages hang from the ceiling ahead.

Use your chopper ability to fly up and smash the two pirate cages.

Fly over and collect the two five-packs of Lums.

Go back to the entrance and fly out into the passage.

Be sure to grab the five-pack of Lums near the tentacles ahead. Throw your magic fist to stun the tentacles and get them out of the way.

When the door ahead of you opens automatically, it's a relief!

You're looking around, excited, not believing you actually made it.

Then the guardian behind you rises up and totally ruins the whole mood.

The guardian knocks you into a pit.

Not only can you not fly anymore, but Foutch the Guardian is hot on your trail.

Dodge the fiery blasts Foutch sends your way.

148

Then start running. Run along the ledges. Jump over the fire waves he throws out, then dodge the fire columns. Bounce on the next cobweb and blast the stalactite with your magic fist.

CAUTION

Avoid the fire columns Foutch throws at any cost. They swirl you up and kill you almost immediately. Time the fire waves he throws at you to time your jumps over gaps. They go together really well if you don't jump too early. It's like they're on a timer and signal when you're supposed to jump the gap.

If you catch Foutch under the stalactite when you cause it to drop, it will drop on his head. Don't stick around to admire your handiwork; keep moving!

After you hit Foutch the third time, he blows apart in a swirl of dust.

Follow the ledges ahead of you.

Turn around at the next overhead bridge to spot the purple Lum.

Throw your magic fist at the purple Lum, then swing up to the bridge.

Walk through the doorway ahead.

Follow the hint marker down into the crevice.

Go through the door ahead, then up the temple steps.

Take the third mask and get whisked away.

After you give the third mask to Polokus, he sends you on your way.

Beneath The Sanctuary of Rock and Stone

Razorbeard is clearly not happy hearing about Rayman's successes.

And you're about to upset the old robo-pirate even more. Take a look at the new world you're in. The door here looks awfully interesting. However, you can't get in there yet.

Turn around and go down the steps.

The next gate has a green Lum behind it.

There's also a note on the wall here.

NOTE

Clark was captured here before being brought to Emission Control.

Leap and glide to the ledge in the lava.

Walk over to the pirate cage. Spot the switch on the wall to the right of the door.

Throw your magic fist to break the cage open, then use it to operate the switch on the wall.

Go back and leap over to the open door.

Go through the door and take the green Lum. Prepare to fight the spider that jumps out at you.

TIP

If at all possible considering your health, it's best to blast this spider now. When you go in the pit later, this guy has a nasty habit of waiting above on the ledge to throw you back down to the spiders waiting in the pit.

You can't jump up on any of the sides, so keep going forward.]

TIP

Beware of all the skull-faced noxious fumes on this level. They do serious damage if you bump into them. Avoid them, or wait for the pauses in between before going through those areas!

Run around the pit ahead to get the Lums there. Watch out for the beak-nosed ghosts.

On the other side of the pit, turn right to spot the line of crates with the piranha leaping over it.

Throw your magic fist at the piranha to blast it away. Continue around the pit and gather the other Lums.

Drop down into the pit and blast the spider. Don't get overly involved in the fights with the spiders because they keep coming.

Leap onto the coffin in the center of the room and hit the switch.

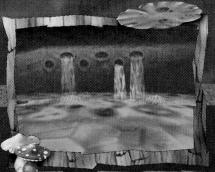

Somewhere in another room, a platform rises up from the murky green water.

Climb up the cobweb to get out of the pit.

Tomb of the Ancients

RAYMAN 2
THE GREAT ESCAPE

Leap across the line of crates where you blasted the piranha.

Enter the opening ahead.

Climb the cobweb to reach the next ledge.

Face the next cobweb on the ledge. Turn left and follow the corridor.

Leap to the next bridge across the lava and keep going.

Put up your magic fist and duke it out with the robo-pirate who pops up on the right. The bridge isn't big, but it gives you enough room to outmaneuver the robo-pirate after all the experience you've gotten.

Take the red Lum that floats out to you from the robo-pirate. Avoid the skeletal claws ahead and leap onto the bone bridge.

Run across the bone bridge, but don't use the chopper ability because it will only slow you down. Leap out to the cobweb and start dodging the spider that joins you.

NOTE

You could have some difficulty with the spider if you hesitate and don't move quickly. It will attack and knock you from its web. You can glide back to the roof-top of the house where the skeletal arm reaches for you and use it to try again. You might think you can stay on this little building and blast the spider, but that's not a good plan. The spider has no problem at all with jumping onto the little building with you. The best advice here is to hurry along the bridge, leap up into the cobweb, and start crawling as soon as you can.

Climb to the right across the cobweb, then up onto the mast with the green Lum to save your progress.

Walk around the mast and spot the switch. Hit it with your magic fist to activate it.

Out in the murky water, another platform rises.

Glide back down to the platform where the robo-pirate showed up, then leap to the bridge and leave this room. Return to the room with the cobweb.

Walk through the door to the right of the cobweb.

Dodge the piranha and walk to the doorway ahead.

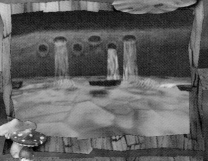

Enter the crypt area but watch out for the skeletal arm that reaches for you. Be aware of the noxious skull-faced fumes here as well. If you dodge the deadly vapors, the center tombs are the safest route.

Blast the robo-pirate who pops up on the right, then look to the left behind the crypts at the back to find a green Lum hiding there.

Turn around to find the switch on the back of the crypt.

Another platform rises in the murky water.

Return to the cobweb and climb up.

At the top of the cobweb-covered ledge, go through the door on the right.

This is definitely one of the windows you saw from the other two rooms you've been through.

The opening on the left a little farther on looks out over the first room you were in.

Tomb of the Ancients

NOTE

The three platforms you raised by flipping the three switches sit in the water before you. If you hadn't found the switches, you'd never be able to cross this water.

Take the green Lum ahead and walk out onto the dock.

Take a close look at the cobweb across the room to spot the hint markers there.

TIP

It's really advisable to blast all the piranha you get near. They'll create all kinds of problems for you along the way if you don't. However, you can dodge and duck them if that's what you want to do.

Leap across the platforms and coffins in the water. Don't jump into the water.

Run across the bone bridges as well.

Leap over to the ledge and climb the cobweb.

Enter the tomb the hint markers are pointing to.

Ahead is a massive gate. Don't jump into the water because it will kill you.

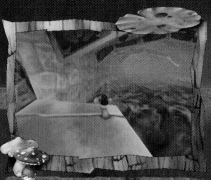

Throw your magic fist at the gears on the right wall to raise the gate. Make sure it goes all the way up so you'll have time to get out of there.

Run around the ledge to the other side.

Jump out onto the barrel in the water there.

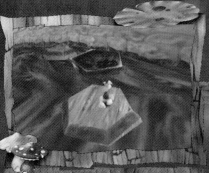

Ride over to the next platform and barrel. Jump out and float over to the platform, then to the next barrel.

Ride the next barrel over the falls.

TIP

When you're making the jumps from barrel to platform to barrel, make sure you're all the way on the other side of each before you jump. Also, the platform goes under the water if you stay on it, so move quickly.

Almost immediately, you're confronted by a robo-pirate firing down at you from the wall.

TIP

If you start firing at the robo-pirate while you're still on the barrel you can hit him and take away nearly half his life before you have to make the jump to the cobweb.

Leap to the cobweb on the left and climb for your life.

Stand in the corner so you can't get blown off the ledge by the robo-pirate's attack. Throw your magic fist at him until he goes to pieces.

Enter the doorway on the left to find an electrified fence. Spot the timed switch on the door to the left.

Throw your magic fist at the timed switch and run through.

Get the green Lum on the ledge ahead of you.

Glide down onto the bridge at the end of the ledge then get moving. The bridge shakes and falls away under you almost instantly.

Run along the ledges and glide down to the floating platforms below.

Tomb of the Ancients

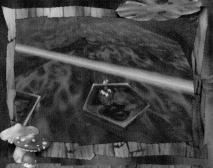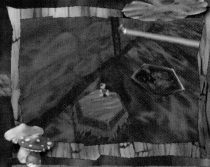

Land on the platform and start jumping. If you stay still, the platform will sink.

Time the electrified bar rising and lowering in front of you. When it goes up, jump under it to the next platform.

Run and leap onto the next barrel.

When the barrel stops, leap into the cobweb ahead. A gate has closed behind you.

Climb the cobweb and work your way to the left and climb down to the boat dock there.

Take the green Lum to save your progress. Then pick up the powder keg on the right and go stand by the torch to ignite it.

Zip out to grab all the yellow Lums spread over the water. Don't aim for the tunnel built high into the wall yet. You'll go there later.

Land on the dock below the tunnel on the wall and turn right to fight the robo-pirate who steps from the doorway there.

NOTE

This doorway leads to the floating barrel section with all the electrified fences later. If you've already gotten the cages and Lums in the area through the tunnel, this doorway can give you a shortcut. Or if you want to end this level in a hurry just to get a look at the next one, you can go through the doorway.

Once the robo-pirate is gone, turn right and walk out onto the short dock.

Look up to spot the cage hanging against the back of the pillar.

Break the cage open with your magic fist and grab the purple Lum inside.

Swing back to the dock with the powder keg and glide down to a safe landing. Grab the powder keg there and step up to the torch again.

Guide the powder keg into the tunnel built high into the wall above the boat dock on the next side.

Walk back along the shaft and drop through the hole in the floor. On the next boat dock you drop to, get the green Lum to save your place.

Take the red Lum and walk around the corner to find another powder keg and torch. From there, guide the powder keg up toward the bridges near the ceiling by weaving around the pillars.

Drop off onto the first bridge near the ceiling.

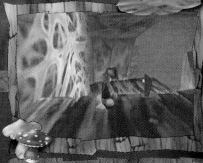

Get all the red Lums here but move quickly because they're on a timer. Turn right and climb along the cobweb to the next bridge. A powder keg is waiting on you.

Fly across to the docks on the other side of the room.

Grab the powder keg and go ignite it at the torch.

Look left to spot the pirate cage hanging under the dock.

Grab the green Lum here but ignore the hole in the dock behind it until you've broken into the cage.

Walk down the other end of the dock by the cage and throw your magic fist into the cage until it breaks. Wait until the 10 yellow Lums in the cage come to you.

Return to the hole in the dock. Blast the robo-pirate who suddenly puts in an appearance here.

Tomb of the Ancients

RAYMAN 2
THE GREAT ESCAPE

Look down into the hole in the dock to find a barrel waiting below. Drop onto the barrel and ride it.

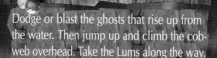

Dodge or blast the ghosts that rise up from the water. Then jump up and climb the cobweb overhead. Take the Lums along the way.

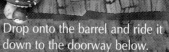

Drop onto the barrel and ride it down to the doorway below.

There are more ghosts to fight along the way, but don't let them distract you from spotting the purple Lum and the pirate cage on the beam along the way. Jump toward it and snare it with your magic fist.

Swing up onto the cobweb on the wall, then climb up onto the beam.

Walk up the beam to spot another purple Lum. You have to jump out and throw your magic fist at this purple Lum to get it. Swing to the other end of the ceiling beam.

Turn left to spot the next purple Lum hanging out over the water. Swing from the first purple Lum here to the next, heading for the ledge against the back wall.

There's one more purple Lum before you reach the back wall. Snag it quickly and keep moving. Grab all the red Lums, then glide down to get the green Lum on the ledge below.

Turn and walk up the beam to break open the pirate cage hanging from the ceiling.

Climb the cobweb at the back but watch out for the spider hanging around there. The spider can be a real pain at this point because not only does it hurt you, it knocks you off the ledge as well. Your best strategy is to leap over the spider and run fast as you can down the corridor behind it.

Fighting the spider is hard in these cramped quarters because the spider can cling to the walls and attack as well. It feels good after you've blasted it away, though.

TIP

If you die somewhere along the way after getting the pirate cage, you don't have to go across the purple Lums again. Simply stay on the barrel and you'll get to the ledge with the green Lum without all the swinging.

Throw your magic fist at the small gear in the middle on the back wall to open the gate. Drop through the hole.

When you land, turn left to spot the door on the ledge. Don't immediately jump for the barrel in front of you.

The problem with this door is that it's guarded by electricity. Go back to the barrel and jump on it.

TIP

You really have to avoid the gassy ghost faces here because they can hurt you and knock you back. Time them to jump on the barrel.

Throw your magic fist at the timed switch on the left wall to avoid being electrified. Grab the yellow Lums along the way and hit the next timed switch to turn off the electricity. Do the same with the third switch as well.

Leap from the first barrel to the second one you spot in the water avoiding the cannonballs whizzing around you. The red Lums actually work as timers, letting you know when it's time to jump back to the other barrel. After you get the red Lum, change barrels again.

Ride the barrel back to the dock and get the green Lum there. Climb the net.

At this point, you're behind the robo-pirate who was firing at you. Watch as the opening you crawled up suddenly becomes electrified and the robo-pirate runs down the stairs. Make sure you get the Lum near the opening.

Move and dodge, and keep pounding the robo-pirate with your magic fist. Use the powder keg against the back wall if you need it.

Look up to spot the purple Lum and the rope ladder leading up to the ceiling. Go up the ladder and to the left to get the purple Lum.

Go get the powder keg in the corner of the lower room and bring it up the stairs to the door with the wooden plank bandage on it.

Blow the door open with the powder keg to reveal the pirate cage. Get the two five-packs of yellow Lums inside.

Tomb of the Ancients

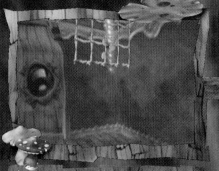

Throw your magic fist out to the purple Lum and swing up to the rope ladder. Drop into the opening on the other side of the ledge at the top.

Follow the corridor around to the Emission Control station. Hit the red switch beside the door to open it.

Enter the room and find Clark huddled against the back wall. At first Clark seems really glad to see you.

Then Clark gets a glazed look in his eyes. It doesn't take a genius to figure out that Clark's under the control of someone else.

If Clark catches you, he can't help himself. He'll hurt you severely.

Throw your magic fist at the three timed switches on poles at the back of this room.

The three switches throw a laser beam across the room. But that doesn't stop Clark. However, if you jump over the laser beam and cause Clark to follow, the laser beam will trip him.

While Clark is sprawled across the floor, shoot the remote control on his back with your magic fist.

Keep turning the laser beam on and tripping Clark so you can blast the control pack. When the control pack is finally blown to bits, Clark is freed.

You also spot the pirate cage on the ceiling. Break it with your magic fist to free the Teensie inside.

The freed Teensie does his victory dance.

A warp gate opens on the floor. Go through the warp gate to return to the Hall of Doors. Enter the Iron Mountains.

The Iron Mountains

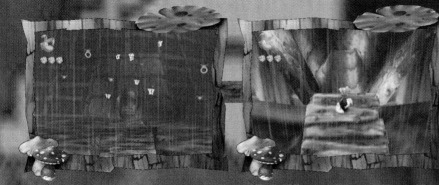

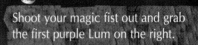

After a brief conversation with the Teensie Council, you're pushed out into the rain. A long bridge stretches out over dark waters, and a forbidding structure lies at the other end.

Once you enter the door at the end of the bridge, you won't be coming back this way unless you die. Return to the end of the bridge by the warp gate.

Shoot your magic fist out and grab the first purple Lum on the right.

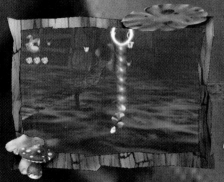

Turn until you face the nearest purple Lum. Throw your magic fist at the purple Lum and swing over to get that yellow Lum. Swing over to the third purple Lum and get the two yellow Lums around it.

Two yellow Lums remain in the sky, with no other purple Lum in sight. Swing out toward the yellow Lums, grabbing them as you leap off the purple Lum and glide down.

Glide to the bridge and enter the tunnel at the end of the bridge. The tunnel twists up again only a little farther on.

Climb the net covering the back of the tunnel.

Swing out on the purple Lum and take a closer look at the turning wheel in the center of the room. Those red beams are lasers and they'll burn you to a crisp. You'll have to jump over them to collect the Lums and to activate the two switches on the walls.

Glide to the left side of the wheel. You can't make it over the laser beam.

TIP
You can jump these laser beams as you come around, but watch falling off the wheel. Getting hit with the laser beam is the lesser of the two evils.

Work your way around the turning wheel to get the Lums, but watch out for the laser beam! If you stand still, the wheel will take you through the Lums, but it will also take you into the laser beam.

Throw your magic fist at the two switches to flip them *down*. Then drop into the open center of the turning wheel after the electrical barrier disappears.

Grab the green Lum ahead to save your progress, then drop into the shaft a little farther on. Once you're on the ground, follow the trail in front of you.

When the robo-pirate jumps up from the ground, throw your magic fist at him and keep dodging until he goes to pieces.

Just after you top the next hill, a second robo-pirate, more powerful than the first, attacks you. Dodge and move and keep hammering away at him.

Walk down the bridge to the building where a magic fist power-up sits. Take the red Lums from the robo-pirate along the way.

Glide to the next section of the bridge and head toward the door at the end. Then enter the tunnel and follow it to a green Lum and a bridge.

Robo-pirates are everywhere in this next area. Keep moving and throwing your magic fist until they're all beaten.

Stand on the small crate by the stacked ones and look up to spot the pirate cage hanging under the bridge.

Climb the stacked crates. Get the yellow Lum at the top. Turn left and glide to the ledge of the building.

Leap up on the ledge to throw your magic fist and hit the pirate crate. Climb the stacked crates and get the yellow Lums, then glide back to the ledge.

Back on the ledge, throw your magic fist at the switch to activate it. Enter the door to the right of the switch.

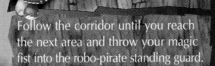

Follow the corridor until you reach the next area and throw your magic fist into the robo-pirate standing guard.

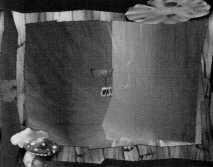

Climb the net ladder on the wall and walk out onto the dam.

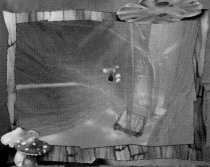

Glide from the dam to the platforms hanging over the river.

Throw your magic fist at the robo-pirate on the platform hanging from the left side of the canyon.

A pirate cage hangs under the platform the robo-pirate was on.

Glide down to the next platform against the right side of the wall. Jump up and throw your magic fist at the pirate cage to break it. Wait for the yellow Lums to come to you.

Glide down the next platforms and work your way around the canyon.

Leap from the last platform in the river and land in the hot air balloon's basket.

NOTE

You have to do a running jump from this last platform, then wait until you sail out for a short distance before using the chopper ability.

Float through the skies with the greatest of ease. Until you jump out.

Don't throw your magic fist at the big-footed monster. You can't hurt it. Race for the crate below the opening in the wall straight ahead.

The Iron Mountains

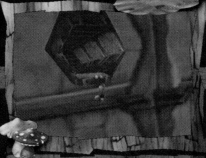

Leap up onto the crate. Even on the crate, you can't reach the opening in the wall. You need just another couple of inches.

Wait until the monster causes the crate to bounce up, then leap off the crate for the opening ahead of you.

TIP

Don't be too close to the edge of the crate or there will be two bounces, first the monster, then you—on the ground.

At the bottom of the ramp, a huge room awaits.

From the fork in the bridge, you'll be able to see the final pirate cage on this level hanging at the end of the overhead bridge.

Take the left fork and read the sign on the wall.

NOTE

Reformatory for disturbing children

Back at the fork, run toward the robo-pirate, then cut to the right and glide to the next bridge.

There's a bouncing crate to your left, but for now turn right and go up the steps. Go up the next set of steps to the right as well.

Walk to the end of the bridge and break the last pirate cage on this level. Take the five-pack of yellow Lums that floats free.

Turn to the right to take the steps down and leap onto the bouncing crate—it'll carry you up to the tunnel in the wall.

Glide into the tunnel in the wall and follow it down.

After you get the green Lum, a walking shell waits at the bottom of the ramp.

Ride the walking shell along the path.

Ignore the left turn and keep going straight. Ride up that pole and you'll find an arrow pointing the way.

Go left, following the path marked by the arrows on the barrels.

Follow the arrows on the wall to make a complete U-turn.

At the end of the long run, turn right and race across the grate.

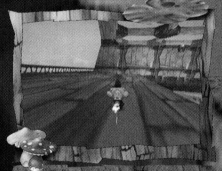

On the other side of the grate, turn right again and keep going.

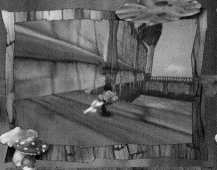

Turn right again and race down the ramp.

Once you're inside the open area, turn right and get up on the wall in front of you to run around and activate the switches.

Duck under the bridge.

Go up on the wall on the opposite side to get the switch there. Also, don't go head-on against the back wall. Get down in the grass then go up on that second wall.

Swing back around and go through the opened doors.

The Iron Mountains

Turn right toward the big-footed monster. Chase him and he'll reveal the yellow Lums under the Stonehenge structure by knocking the stones over.

All four Stonehenge pieces have yellow Lums under them. Circle around the big-footed monster and chase him into the stones to get all of them.

Line back up with the building on your left and streak across the land.

There's another building ahead in the distance.

Ride the walking shell across the bridge and jump off.

Walk into the caverns.

Race across the new area.

Now that's a disgusting look with all the toxic water out there. However, the plums that bounce by look inviting.

Line up with the crate out in the middle of the water and glide out to it.

Catch a plum, then turn around and toss it to shore. Run after it quickly before it has the chance to bounce back into the water.

Pick the plum up and toss it farther back over the next ledge. Get to it before it can bounce off the ledge or you have to do it again.

NOTE

Your original assumption in this place is that you need the plum to get through the water. Notice that every time a plum touches the water it disintegrates. Not a good sign, and the proof's in the (plum) pudding.

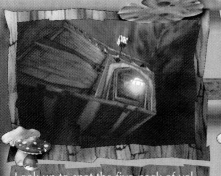

Look up to spot the five-pack of yellow Lums hiding by the door. Throw the plum straight up near the Lum, then leap up onto the plum. Leap up again to get your prize.

Stand on the left side of your screen facing the big tower. Look up to spot the purple Lum there. Jump up and throw your magic fist at the purple Lum.

Swing up on top of the pipe leading from the tower.

Leap on top of the tower to find another five-pack of yellow Lums on the other side.

TIP

You can't glide to get onto the tower's pipe. You fall short every time. Get to the highest point of your swing, then leap and flip to land on the pipe.

Glide down to get the yellow Lum. Land on the pipe below.

Turn around and glide for the ship.

Land on the ship's deck.

Turn and glide to the bridge.

Leap the gap and enter the mine door ahead.

Walk to the back of the tunnel to find another bridge.

Turn right and walk along this bridge. Jump over the gap and keep going.

The Iron Mountains

Grab the green Lum ahead and look at all the trouble you're about to head into.

Keep leaping and running along the bridge and you'll find a Uglette crying over her missing babies.

After finding out Globox is imprisoned in the pirate ship and the babies have been taken to the mines, Rayman confiscates a nearby pirate ship and sets out to save them.

Of course, he immediately runs into dangerous waters.

TIP

All you have to do in this part of the game is keep the ship between the canyon walls and break through the barriers ahead.

The rescue at the South Mine goes off without a hitch.

Get underway again. Fire at the bridge ahead to break it down. Use your magic fist as usual to fire pink blasts from the top of the mast.

When you come to the fork, go to the left side and dodge the poles.

Dock at the West Mine on the left to complete another rescue.

Then dock at the North Mine on the left.

Blast through the next barrier.

Sail to the second right of the next tower. Don't take the first canyon to the right; it has to be the second or you'll crack up and die.

This canyon is really narrow, so sail carefully.

A short distance farther you'll find the West Mine again. You're now going back the way you came.

You'll pass the North Mine on the left next.

Take the next left when you spot the familiar tower ahead. It's at the fork where you took the left the first time. Now you're coming out of the right fork.

Find the two entrances that lie side by side and go through the right to get to the East Mine. Turn around at the end of this passage and sail back out to the central area where all the passages lead from. Turn at the first left and sail back to Uglette.

When you get back to Uglette, she's depressed and sitting on the ledge where you left her.

All the babies you rescued spill off the ship and run to their mom.

One of the babies has even brought the fourth mask of Polokus.

After the Globox clan leaves, the mask takes you to Polokus. He fits the last mask into place.

Polokus floats up on his pillar and works his magic.

Polokus opens a new warp that will take you to the pirate prison ship.

Polokus goes back to sitting quietly. He's done his part. Now it's up to you.

The Iron Mountains

The Prison Ship

Captain Razorbeard has sent out for reinforcements, who have come up with the ultimate weapon. It's called the Grolgoth.

Razorbeard instantly decides to purchase the vicious automaton.

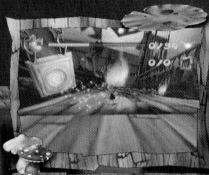

This level begins with a bang, and if you're not careful, you're the bang!

Grab the Lums as you go whizzing by on the slippery deck, but watch out for the flames.

Use the uneven places in the ship's deck like waves. Change directions by taking advantage of those even places to switch back and forth across the deck more easily.

TIP
Pull down on the control stick to slow your speed and get a little more control.

You have to jump over the small bump in the deck to grab the Lum beside the windmill. Otherwise you'll overshoot it every time.

Once you get into the next section of the slide, you'll have to throw your magic fist into the switch on the right to deactivate the deadly laser beams covering the doorway ahead.

Leap up to avoid the exploding deck sections, then jump the gap and keep going.

NOTE

It's going to take a number of trips through this level to get all the Lums, so for now just hunker down and try to get to the end.

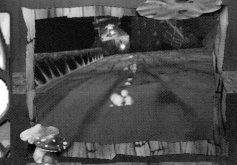

Shoot the next switch to the left of the spiked pole.

A ramp drops into place to the left of the spiked pole. Go up it.

Another switch on the left needs to be activated.

Once you activate it, a ramp opens beneath the switch that allows you to miss the turning spiked pole.

The next switch you have to hit lowers another ramp to go over.

Throw your magic fist at the next switch on the left to drop a ramp there.

Stay on the ramp after the next jump.

Go around the hole in the floor to gather the Lums there. Then go down into the hole.

The console in front of you looks interesting, but there's nothing you can do with it. Walk in front of it.

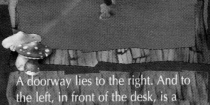

A doorway lies to the right. And to the left, in front of the desk, is a teleporter unit. Walk through the doorway and out onto the catwalk.

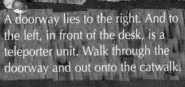

The Prison Ship

There's a door on the other side of the room, but you can't get there like this. Jump forward from the end of the catwalk.

Glide down to the ledge on the right that has crates on it.

Duck and dodge and blast the robo-pirate on guard here.

Throw your magic fist at the switch on the wall.

Climb the catwalk. Then turn left and glide out to the ledge with the magic fist power-up.

Climb the catwalk again and up to the tallest ledge along the chains at the back.

Look down at this catwalk directly behind the spiked roller to spot the five-pack of yellow Lums hiding there. You can't get it yet, but you will.

Take the yellow Lum in the corner and walk back to the teleporter in front of the desk.

A walking shell races from the teleporter, all revved up and ready to go. Saddle up cowboy!

Aim for the doorway on the other side of the room. Gather the yellow Lums that are scattered under the bridges and between the big tanks.

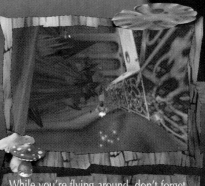

While you're flying around, don't forget about the five-pack of yellow Lums you spotted behind the spiked roller under the catwalk. Fly back out into the open.

The switch that opens the door at the other end of the room can be hard to spot. It's on the short catwalk leading to the closed door.

Once you're through the open door, keep flying.

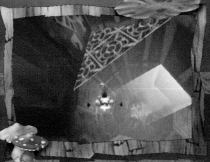

A closed door ahead promises certain death—you'll smash like a bug on a windshield.

Make sure you're right side up as you swoop toward the door. Look to the left to spot the opening. Fly through it.

Keep grabbing the trail of yellow Lums.

Fly under the gap at the bottom of the big skull door on the other side of the room.

Fly up the stairs above the net hanging on the wall. Then dive under the next skull-faced door.

Fly along the corridor.

Follow the next line of red steps.

Fly through the beams ahead. Keep a loose touch on the control stick and don't make any sudden moves.

Follow the line of red Lums to another twist of crossed beams that lies ahead. Navigate your way through them as well.

Once you fight your way free of the beams and enter a dark corridor, you're assaulted by laser beams.

Enter the door at the end of this corridor to get into the interior of the ship.

The Prison Ship

Wind your way through the next corridor that's filled with crisscrossed beams. Bear to the left because the right side ends in a wall just a little farther on.

One of Razorbeard's flunkies has to tell him that you've penetrated the ship's defenses.

Razorbeard knows he has to take matters into his own hands.

The pirate ship hangs over the world, but everything is about to break loose. Captain Razorbeard pulls out his secret weapon.

In only a short time, Razorbeard has put his evil plan into effect.

Seated inside the huge Grolgoth, Razorbeard sets his sights on you.

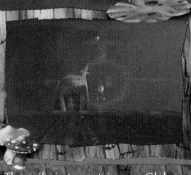

The evil pirate captain uses Globox as a hostage.

Once you and Razorbeard square off on the battleground, it's doomsday! He topples the structure Globox is hanging from.

Globox hangs precariously from the toppled structure. There's no time to lose now.

Razorbeard hurls three explosives at a time at you.

Run around the makeshift battleground to get some maneuvering room. Beware of the edges or you'll fall to your death.

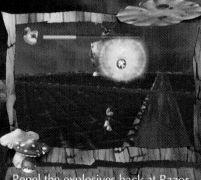

Repel the explosives back at Razorbeard by throwing your magic fist into them.

NOTE

Razorbeard's usual attack consists of throwing the explosives then jumping on you. When you hit him, he shifts to fiery blasts from his feet that you need to avoid, followed by the big jump attack.

Hit Razorbeard to topple him. He will dodge sometimes, so make sure you get a good spread on the three explosives by shifting before throwing your magic fist at each of them. It takes a little practice, but you'll master it quickly.

After you hit Razorbeard three times, you won't completely finish him, but you will make him terribly angry. He jumps at you again, but this time he plunges through the decking.

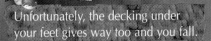

In the forest, Ly hears your screams for help and contacts you.

Unfortunately, the decking under your feet gives way too and you fall.

Even as you're falling, you spot the silver Lum she's sent to help you. Ain't magic great!

It does look like certain doom is waiting for you in the lava pit but the silver Lum halts your fall, floating you safely above the lava.

In seconds, you're transported to safe ground inside the battleground where you're joined by a walking shell that's totally excited to see you.

Ly speaks to you with her magic, telling you Razorbeard still has to be destroyed even though the robo-pirates have all been beaten on the planet.

Unbelievably, Razorbeard and the Grolgoth have survived. Even with one leg blown off, the evil pirate captain has managed to catch himself between two support poles.

Hanging there with his pet robot all beat up, Razorbeard still won't give up. Fly over the lava. Dropping into it will kill you.

Part of Razorbeard's arsenal includes heat-seeking missiles. They only last for a short time. Stay ahead of them, then when they start to close on you, pull a 180-degree turn to shake them loose.

The Prison Ship

STRATEGY

Two tunnels branch off the main chamber where Razorbeard hangs. A cannon appears in them, in alternating places so you have to go search for it. Just fly by it to acquire it. The cannon has four shots, so use them well. Once you use them up, the cannon disappears and you have to go get another one.

Use two of the four shots in a single pass on the Grolgoth's hands to drop it into the lava. You'll have to turn slightly from side to side to enable the auto-aiming feature to work. Save the final two cannon rounds to hit Razorbeard while he's flailing around in the lava to do maximum damage.

It'll take three or four passes to completely put him down. When you shoot the Grolgoth's hands, pull up and fly into the tunnel above it to do a 180-degree turn and come straight back down at him.

When you've got Razorbeard down to the last little bit of his life, he'll scramble up into this upper passage and attempt to hide. You'll have to go after him and knock him down again.

As soon as you've destroyed the Grolgoth, Razorbeard flies from the robot in a small aircraft.

Razorbeard tells you it isn't over yet. He has a final surprise for you. As he flies away, you get a really bad feeling.

The explosives Razorbeard has planted throughout the pirate ship suddenly rip it to shreds in the air.

Ly sits on her branch afterward. It's easy to see she's sad. Everyone else is sad, too.

It seems that all that was found of Rayman after the huge explosion was one lone foot.

Then, out of the shadows, supported on a crutch, comes our hero.

Everyone goes from sad to glad!

Ly is satisfied, happy that all is right with the world again.

THE END

But have you really seen the last of the evil pirate captain? Razorbeard may still be lurking out there somewhere, putting together his next evil plans!